HAUNTED TOO

HAUNTED TOO

Incredible True Stories of
Ghostly Encounters

Dorah L. Williams

DUNDURN
TORONTO

Editor: Andrea Waters
Design: Courtney Horner
Printer: Webcom

Library and Archives Canada Cataloguing in Publication

Williams, Dorah L.
        Haunted too : incredible true stories of ghostly encounters
/ Dorah L. Williams.

Also issued in electronic format.
ISBN 978-1-4597-0608-8

        1. Ghosts. I. Title.

BF1461.W545 2012   133.1   C2012-903206-9

1   2   3   4   5   16   15   14   13   12

Conseil des Arts du Canada   Canada Council for the Arts   Canada   ONTARIO ARTS COUNCIL CONSEIL DES ARTS DE L'ONTARIO

We acknowledge the support of the **Canada Council for the Arts** and the **Ontario Arts Council** for our publishing program. We also acknowledge the financial support of the **Government of Canada** through the **Canada Book Fund** and **Livres Canada Books**, and the **Government of Ontario** through the **Ontario Book Publishing Tax Credit** and the **Ontario Media Development Corporation**.

Care has been taken to trace the ownership of copyright material used in this book. The author and the publisher welcome any information enabling them to rectify any references or credits in subsequent editions.
                                                                    J. Kirk Howard, President

Printed and bound in Canada.
www.dundurn.com

Dundurn
3 Church Street, Suite 500
Toronto, Ontario, Canada
M5E 1M2

Gazelle Book Services Limited
White Cross Mills
High Town, Lancaster, England
LA1 4XS

Dundurn
2250 Military Road
Tonawanda, NY
U.S.A. 14150

*This book is dedicated
to Sylvia.*

*And in memory of Leslie,
forever in our hearts.*

Contents

Acknowledgements

I know how it feels to be haunted. And I also understand that when it happens, you want, or even feel a need, to talk about it. But ridicule or disbelief may be the response you receive from anyone who has not had a similar experience. That often causes an understandable reluctance to discuss paranormal encounters. But if you have had something similar happen, you can relate to a ghost story much better and know if it rings true.

Even if one is not able to relate, hearing what phenomena others have witnessed might replace one's fear of the unknown with an awe of what might be and a more open mind.

So I would very much like to express my gratitude to everyone who shared their personal hauntings in this book. Nothing describes a ghostly encounter better than a first-hand account, because paranormal events are so emotionally charged they seem to produce "flashbulb" memories when they occur. Whether it happened in the past few days or several decades ago, that memory will likely forever remain vivid and therefore can be clearly depicted.

I also greatly appreciate the input of all the paranormal investigators and mediums. They were chosen from across Canada, the United States, and the United Kingdom to give their perspectives based on their own personal and professional experiences.

———

From Canada:

Heather Anderson — executive director for the western region of Paranormal Studies and Investigations Canada

Rona Anderson — paranormal investigator and psychic medium, The Paranormal Explorers, Edmonton, Alberta

Peter Clayton — author and student of the shamanic journey, Ontario

Dave Gibb, John Tallon, and Lisa Carter — paranormal investigators, Canadian Haunting and Paranormal Society, Ontario

Scott Hobbs — paranormal investigator, the Thunder Bay Paranormal Society, Ontario

Kimberley Lapierre, Nicki Himmelman, and Lynsey Robson — paranormal investigators, Light Workers Paranormal Investigation, Nova Scotia

———

From the United States:

Jill Bruener — medium, clairvoyant, spiritual and psychic advisor of Paranormal Investigators of Northern Kentucky, and weekly guest for over ten years on two of Cincinnati's top morning shows

Jamie Jackson — paranormal investigator, Gettysburg Ghosts, Gettysburg, Pennsylvania

Ian Murphy — paranormal investigator, Paranormal Research Association of Boston

Dr. Dave Oester — co-founder of International Ghost Hunters Society, with Dr. Sharon Oester

Don Swain and Linda Swain — paranormal investigators, Yuma, Arizona

———

From the United Kingdom:

Barri Ghai — paranormal investigator, The Ghostfinder Paranormal Society, London, England

Julie Harwood, Stephen Boston, Wendy Callaway, Amanda Horley, Marie Holder, Sarah Pettet, and Maria Street — paranormal investigators, Southern Paranormal UK

Introduction

Several years ago, my family and I lived in an old house that was very haunted, with apparitions, apports (objects that suddenly appeared out of thin air), ghostly handprints, voices and touches, and so many other paranormal phenomena that it felt almost overwhelming at times, and had quite an impact on all of us. But the more I researched and discussed this topic with others, the less afraid I became. My fear was replaced with a new appreciation and awe for what I have witnessed.

When I wrote *Haunted: The Incredible True Story of a Canadian Family's Experience Living in a Haunted House*, I thought our situation was unique. I had no idea how many others who also live with or have experienced a haunting would contact me. And the more people who did, the more I came to realize that encounters with spirits are not uncommon at all. This compilation of others' encounters, followed by insight, advice, and paranormal experiences from those with careers in this field, show that hauntings can occur anywhere, and to anyone.

I have been emailed by people from around the world, and from all walks of life, seeking information to better understand their own experiences. Most of them expressed the same fears and confusion that I felt myself when trying to come to terms with what was happening.

When I first realized our house was haunted, I felt at a loss as to what to do in a situation that felt so surreal. I understand the awe, bewilderment, or fright that others expressed to me regarding the hauntings they were trying to comprehend. And some felt they had no other option than to sell their homes and move away. But because all I could offer was advice based on my own specific, limited personal experience, I realized the need was there for more in-depth information from people who are a lot more knowledgeable than I am.

So I went looking for answers to the questions that people kept asking me when trying to understand their ghostly experiences — the same questions I had asked while our haunting was at its peak. I turned to paranormal investigators, researchers, and psychics, who were very generous with their time and knowledge, and I have compiled the information I felt was most needed.

Basic human nature causes most people to enjoy a good ghost story, because we somehow like the sensation of being frightened. There is an adrenaline rush caused by fear that, on varying levels, most people want to experience, if only vicariously from the safety of their seat in a movie theatre or within the pages of a book. But it feels much different when it is actually happening to you. Then the fear or amazement are not caused by someone else's imagination or experience, but by your own reality. And closing a book or walking out of a movie theatre won't stop the real-life drama that is unfolding in your home.

So this book has been written for two purposes. One is to share what others have felt and learned from their own paranormal experiences. And the other is to enlighten and intrigue anyone who would enjoy a vicarious "haunting" or spiritual uplifting.

Whether frightening or poignant, these paranormal incidents are told first-hand by those who have had them. Positive or negative, these remarkable experiences made a lasting impression on them, and they felt others might enjoy or learn from hearing their stories. And so do I.

1

THE HAUNTED EXPERIENCES OF OTHERS IN CANADA

WESTERN CANADA

BEHIND THE WALL

Quite a few years ago I lived in the attic apartment of a very old and grand Victorian-era house. By the time I moved out of there I was a firm believer in ghosts.

I rented the attic in what was a four-plex, with tenants also living on the first two floors and one in the basement. When I first saw the apartment's advertisement in the newspaper asking such a low rental price, I thought it must be located in a less than desirable area of the city. To my surprise, though, the neighbourhood was actually in a great location, and one that I had always admired. Even a century after the house was first built, and after it was turned from a single-family home into apartments, it still had an air of elegance about it. I knew the rental market well, and I could not understand why an apartment in a building and location such as that would be so inexpensive, but I felt very fortunate to have found it and happily signed the lease and moved in at the beginning of the following month.

I loved my new apartment and immediately felt at home. If it hadn't been for a strange recurring nightmare I started to have right after moving in there, everything would have been perfect.

But the dreams were really frightening, and I couldn't understand what was causing them, because I had never had nightmares like that before in my life (or since).

The dream always began with me climbing the stairs to my apartment as I returned home from work at the end of the day, and felt more lifelike than dreams normally do. As I approached the apartment I could hear a young woman crying uncontrollably, and would frantically fumble for my keys, trying to get the door open to see who was inside my apartment and why they were crying like that. But every time the door was opened the sobbing would immediately stop and an eerie silence hung in the air.

At first that was all I would dream. I would wake up and think I could almost still hear the crying in the darkness around me. But eventually, after a few weeks, the action in the dream would continue. After entering the apartment I would realize the woman's crying was coming from a closet in the living room. I would open the closet door and search frantically through it trying to find her to help.

One night, in my dream, I started to rip out the shelves and pry the drywall off of the back of the closet, as the woman's cries behind the wall started to become a high-pitched scream. Just as I was about to pull out a part of the wall and peer through the opening, I woke up in bed.

For whatever reason, after recurring all those weeks, the nightmares suddenly stopped and I never had that dream again. But the closet in my living room made me feel really uncomfortable, even after the dreams had ended, and the only thing I used it for was to store my winter clothing.

My friends all liked my new home, but several of them pointed out that the size of the apartment's interior did not seem to compare to the dimensions of the building's third-storey exterior. In fact, it seemed like an area about the size of a bedroom was not accounted for, and again I realized that closet seemed to be the cause.

There was a large unaccounted-for area between the living room and my bedroom. The door to the closet seemed to have led into a much larger space at one time, but now it was an area of only a few square feet. This reminded me of the dream, of course, and it did seem obvious that there really was some kind of space, if not a specific room, boarded up behind that closet.

Once I came home from the beach with two of my friends on a really hot summer day. We had planned to meet another friend at my apartment. When we entered the house's front foyer I saw, through the railing, someone sitting near the bottom of the stairway, which faced the other direction. I assumed it was our friend and called out a greeting to her and told her that we would be there in a minute as soon as we unloaded the car. There was no reply. So while my other two friends brought in the cooler and blankets I went toward the stairway and the person sitting there. As I walked down the hallway toward the foot of the stairs, I passed the profile of the female figure sitting on the third or fourth step from the bottom. Through the railing's spindles I saw, and even brushed against, her abundance of heavy clothing. I could see the woman was wearing layer upon layer of long woollen skirts and petticoats. And this fact alone, on such a sweltering day, bewildered me. With my hand on the railing and my eye looking in the direction of where the woman was sitting only a few feet away, I pivoted myself around the large newel post, so that I was then facing the stairway. As I did that, I asked my friend why she was wearing so many clothes on such a hot summer afternoon. But within the second or two that it took for me to spin myself around that post to face the stairway, the woman sitting there had completely vanished.

I couldn't stop staring at the empty stairway, and it took a few minutes for the reality of what had just happened to make an impact. I had just assumed it was my friend waiting for us on the stairs. But, obviously it had not been. She arrived a few minutes later, and was wearing shorts and a tank top.

The woman I saw, I realized, was dressed in fashions from the previous century. But it wasn't her clothing that was even so startling as the fact that she simply disappeared into thin air. She had looked completely solid, like a normal person, which is why I had mistaken her for my friend. The coarse fabric of her woollen skirt protruded through the railing spindles, and I had even felt it scratch against my sensitive sunburned arms as I walked past the stairwell.

There were only two exits from that particular stairway: one was my locked apartment at the top of the stairs, and the other was out the front door of the house. But my friends and I knew that no one rushed past us in the hallway that day. Whoever had been sitting on those stairs simply disappeared.

I never saw her again, but I know I felt her a few months later. My relationship with my boyfriend had just ended, and I was very upset one day and lay crying on my bed shortly after he had left. I was sobbing, with my face buried into my pillows, when I suddenly felt the bed sag beside me, as though someone had just sat down. Then a hand very gently began to pat the top of one of my hands, as if to console me. I froze. I understood, even through my fear, that whoever it was didn't mean to scare me, only comfort me as I cried. But it did terrify me. I was afraid to look up from the pillow, where my face was still buried, but I wanted to flee. I grabbed my hand away from the patting and shoved it under the pillow out of reach, and said, as calmly as I could make myself sound, "I'm okay now, please leave me alone"… and she did.

At the end of the year I learned that the Victorian house was being sold. The new owner wanted to convert the building back to its original state, as a single family home, and live in it himself. The tenants were all given notice that we would have to move. This was very upsetting news to me; I really loved living in that old house.

The day before I moved, I returned home from work to discover that the new owner had been in my apartment while I had been gone that day. He had mentioned to me that he needed to take some measurements for the renovation, but I thought he meant for the windows. Now I saw that the heavy wooden shelves from the closet in the living room had been removed and were leaning up against the wall beside it.

I slowly approached the closet and nervously opened the door. A large hole had been cut into the back wall, and a string, from a ceiling light in the area beyond, hung through the opening. Even before I pulled the string to turn on the light I could see into the darkness well enough to make out that there was a large room hidden behind the closet: just like in my dream when I was trying to get to the crying woman behind the wall.

The light bulb must have been very old, but still dimly lit the room. I peered through the hole in the wall and saw that it had once been a bedroom. The hole was not large enough for me to see the whole area, but I could clearly see that the furniture had all been left in place when the room had been sealed up as it was.

I couldn't understand why anyone would board up a furnished bedroom like that. But in that recurring nightmare that haunted me for so many weeks, there was a woman crying behind the wall of that closet. And the woman sitting on the stairs was dressed in clothing from the same era in which I would estimate the bedroom had last been used.

There must have been an explanation for all of this, but I had to move out of the apartment the following day and was never able to learn any more about it.

HER FRIEND ELGIN

When our daughter was about two years old, she would talk about her friend "Elgin," who played with her and came to see her at night before she went to sleep. She had begun to talk at a very early age and was very fluent and articulate by that point.

She said he had white hair and a white beard and his clothes were black. We had no idea what or who she was talking about and had never even heard of anyone with that name before (so she hadn't overheard us ever discussing someone called Elgin and parroted that name).

One day I was in the library and doing some research to see what I could learn about our house. I wasn't even thinking about our daughter's invisible friend; I was just curious to see what I could find out about our ninety-year-old home's history.

Well, I discovered that a man named Elgin had owned the property for a long time, shortly after it was built, until the previous owner, who had sold to us, bought it from him. He had spent most of his long life in that house. And I found a photograph of him in the library. I showed it to my daughter and said, "Who is this?"

She smiled when she saw it, and said "That's Elgin!"

———————

THERE'S NO PLACE LIKE HOME

Our house has had some sad history, and that might account for the things we have experienced while living here, if, as they say, untimely deaths cause spirits to remain earthbound.

When it was built in the mid-1800s it was a modest one-storey house. But as the original owner prospered he kept adding on to the house until it was built into the large home it is today.

He started out as a small local merchant but soon owned many businesses in town. He had immigrated to Canada from England with his parents as a small boy, and in the 1881 census his elderly widowed mother is listed as living with him and his wife and their five surviving children in this house.

I found some information about this family in the library archives, and many more records were found on Internet genealogy sites.

I learned that he and his bride moved into their new house at the time of their marriage, when it was still just the small original structure. Two years later she died of influenza. And their infant daughter also died of that just a few days later.

He remarried five years after that, and had six children with his second wife. Their eldest son was killed when he fell down the steep cellar stairs and broke his neck when he was only ten.

When his second wife died in 1895, he sold the house. We bought it a few years ago, after many other owners, and have done an extensive restoration on it.

So ... that brings me up to the haunting part. As I said, we have extensively restored the house and while doing so we had many people working on it with us for months. So during all that chaos I didn't notice anything out of the ordinary. It wasn't until we were actually living in the house that it began, or at least became noticeable.

At first it was nothing definite, just feelings like being watched. Sometimes it feels like you hit a pocket of icy cold air as you walk in a certain area of the house. But as it is a very old house, drafts are to be expected in colder months. In the summertime, with no central air in the house, those icy pockets of air are a bit more difficult to explain. That never scares anyone; it's just a weird thing that often happens.

And then there are the strange sounds; but again, in a very old house that is not completely unexpected either. When doors open or close and floorboards creak we just try to ignore it as being due to the house's age.

But there is also a distinctive little boy's voice and laughter. We've all heard it, and usually when we're all together in the same room, so we know it isn't anyone else in the family.

We've also heard the sound of running. It always starts in the upstairs sunroom area and travels along the hallway and down the back stairway into the kitchen. It's the laughing that is most often heard, though, and we've also clearly heard a little boy call out, "Papa" and "in here."

Another odd thing, to do with voices too, is that a few times my daughter has come looking for me to see why I called her, when I never did. But she heard someone calling her and thought it was me.

My husband is the only person, so far, who has actually seen a ghost in our house. And this has happened to him twice. One evening, when he was the only one at home, he walked up the stairs toward our bedroom after getting home late from work. Through the railing, he thought he saw me, in my nightgown, walking through the doorway into our room. As he continued up the rest of the stairway he asked why I hadn't gone to the movie with my daughter as planned. When there was no answer, and he was alone when he walked into the bedroom, he realized whomever he had seen was gone. But he was positive he saw a woman going into that room, and thought it must be me.

When I got home later he was still a bit dumbfounded at what he had seen.

The second time he saw something it scared him a bit more. Again, it was when he was there alone. He had just arrived home from work and came in through the back way. Our dog went to greet him, and as he was taking off his coat and walking toward the front entrance to hang it up, he saw someone, or something, very large come right through the closed front door. He said a red mass (like a mist) came through the solid oak door and then started to form into a very tall man. The dog yelped and hid behind my husband (some watchdog). He stared at it for a few seconds as it took a human shape, and then it dissolved into thin air.

In spite of the haunting, we love living here. This house felt special right from the start, and the longer we live here the deeper I feel the connection with it. I can understand why past residents might want to remain.

HAUNTED GROUND

My experience isn't really about a haunted house so much as about the land the house was built on.

My husband and I were very excited about the new house we were going to build when we sold our old house. The only problem was that we had a really hard time finding a building lot to purchase. We had two small children and hoped to build in a quiet area of the city, but not many lots were available at that time. Finally we had it narrowed down to three possible lots, but two were in areas that we really didn't like and the third was about twice the price we wanted to pay. But we had to make a decision fairly quickly, because the house's construction had to start so it would be ready to move into by the time our old house had to be vacated.

We decided to go with the expensive lot, even though it cost a lot more than our initial budget had allowed. It was a beautiful piece of property with gorgeous, mature trees, on a really quiet street. And something that we also really liked was that it was right beside an incredible 1800s-era mansion that sat on a huge estate-sized lot that took up the rest of the block.

So as we drove by the property, it seemed like, other than the price, it would be an ideal place to build our house and raise our family. But once the car was parked and we started to walk around the property I suddenly became violently ill. I had been feeling well, with no sign of sickness, right up until that moment. It just hit me full force right out of the blue. I was so sick that we headed back to the car as soon as I could make it that far and planned to go right back to our house. As soon as I got back into the car I was fine again, but we left anyway in case the illness returned. It didn't. I felt completely normal still when we got home, and remained well until we went back to the building site the following week. Although not quite as intense as the first time, I was sick again as soon as I started to walk onto the property. We had not considered that the property could somehow be the cause of the illness at that point, but once again the minute I walked off the property and sat in the car, parked on the road, I immediately felt fine. I had so much to do during that time period that being sick was the last thing I needed, so I was very relieved when the feeling passed so quickly and I was able to resume my busy schedule when I got back home.

A few days later my husband suggested we drive by the building site again to see how the work on the new house was coming along. By then, though, I was starting to sense that for some bizarre reason that property made me feel deathly ill whenever I walked on it. This was a terrible feeling, because our new house was being built on that lot and I knew I couldn't avoid it forever. So, somewhat nervously, we drove over to the new property. I sat in the car for a few minutes before I felt ready to walk over to where the house was being built. Nothing happened at first, and I was relieved and felt foolish at the same time. I thought it had been pretty ridiculous that I had thought there was any connection between that land and my recent bouts of illness.

We stayed for a while. I didn't feel sick to my stomach and was very relieved about that, but did notice a strange but obvious tension started to develop between my husband and me. We have always had a great relationship and are the best of friends, but as we stood looking at the foundation hole that had been dug and the other work that was being done, we started snapping at each other over the most trivial things. This was so out of character for us that it must have almost sounded funny, but at the time I felt this very real fury at him, but couldn't really understand why. I could tell from his tone that he was furious at me too, and we acted like we were enemies. It was lucky our kids were at home with a babysitter because I wouldn't have wanted them to hear their parents talking to each other like that!

We made up by the time we got home and both felt terrible for how we had treated each other. Like my illness, the negative feelings we had toward each other had just come out of nowhere and left just as quickly as soon as we left the property.

By the time our house was finished it looked great and we were all happy with it. Everything seemed fine for the first few weeks, but then our youngest child became really ill. After consulting several doctors, including specialists, no one could ever determine what was causing the problem. Eventually everything was fine again, and fortunately the illness did not return and everyone remained healthy. But that awful tension definitely came back into our marriage. We were so miserable for the whole time we lived in that house.

After a couple of years my husband was offered a new job and we had to move. When the real estate agent was over to give us an appraisal on what the property was worth, he remarked on what a huge improvement our next-door neighbours had made to their home. I was curious about that, because their house was so beautiful and I had only ever known it to look like that. He explained to me that a long time ago (probably at least fifty years), when he was a young boy, he had lived nearby, and he and the other neighbourhood children used to bet each other that they wouldn't have the nerve to step onto the "haunted" house's property, because they were all terrified of that whole area.

At that time the property was completely overgrown, and the mansion was in a terrible state of disrepair because it had long been abandoned. The property that our house was built on was originally part of that huge estate. But the house next door was now beautifully restored and didn't look anything like the agent remembered. I asked him why it had the reputation of being haunted, but he seemed very reluctant to talk about it further and the topic was dropped. And I never did learn any more about the history of that property before we moved.

What I did learn, though, through friends in the neighbourhood, was that since we left, just a few years ago, the house has had a very high turnover rate, with the next two couples who owned it after us both leaving shortly after they moved in, on account of their marriages breaking up and them getting divorced. And the next owner, a single middle-aged woman, had some sort of nervous breakdown after living there for only a few months, and had to move away to live with her father in another city.

So after that experience, I truly believe now that even if you build a new house that no one else has lived in before, it can still be "haunted" by whatever negative energy the property it is built on, has, especially if there was a disturbing history of some kind.

———

SWEATER GIRL

I don't know if this could be classified as a ghost story, because I'm not sure it was a ghost that I saw. That experience definitely haunted me, though, and whatever it was, it could only be described as supernatural.

About twenty years ago, when my youngest child had just turned one, we moved to a new town and bought our first house there, in the oldest (and busiest) section of town.

The only problem I had with the neighbourhood was the congestion from all the traffic on a street not designed to accommodate modern vehicles. Between three-thirty and four o'clock every afternoon, dismissed students from four different schools in the area surrounding us hurried past, and even inside our house the noise from this was very loud.

One warm, sunny spring day I was playing with my little daughter in our living room. She would get so excited to see all the children racing by at dismissal time that I would sometimes put her into her playpen in front of the large bay window so she could happily watch them.

The traffic started to increase as always, with parents approaching the schools to pick up their children, and I could hear the bells start to ring, signalling another ended school day. And on cue, as always, the kids not getting rides started walking or running down the street, free from school for the rest of the day. So, in every way, it just seemed like a very typical afternoon.

But as I placed the baby into her playpen for a better view of all this commotion, something happened that I will never, ever forget. The sunny afternoon suddenly (and when I say suddenly I do mean *immediately*) turned into a cold, cloudy day. And although there had been a constant din of noise and activity right outside the window up until that very second, it was now deathly silent, without a vehicle or person in sight. Even my neighbour who had seen me looking out the window and had just waved to me from his front garden only a moment before was no longer visible.

My daughter stared up at me, and her big blue eyes showed just as much bewilderment as I was feeling myself. I walked over to the front door and slowly turned the knob, feeling I had to investigate what was going on, but nervous to leave the safety of my home. I glanced back at the baby in her playpen, and then immediately looked in the large front window at her again as soon as I stepped out onto the porch so she knew I was still there.

We were both baffled. I stood on our front porch staring up and down the street trying to understand how the cloudless, sunny day had been so altered so quickly into the cold, damp grey afternoon it now was. But, even more so, I tried to make sense out of how everyone else on the street had completely disappeared, including all the vehicles. No children, no parents, no neighbours, no cars or bikes. In fact, one of my neighbours had been cutting some limbs in his backyard, and I realized then that even that noise from the chainsaw had been eliminated. It was completely and eerily silent.

And then I saw her. As I stared up the street, looking for even one school kid, when there should have been dozens, I saw a lone figure walking slowly toward my house. I stared at her with relief at first … at least there was another person, and surely, I thought, more would start to fill the street again soon, as usual. But the silence remained, and the odd chill in the air made me rub my bare arms with my hands, trying to warm them. I kept glancing in the window at the baby, and she kept her eyes fixed on me the whole time. I'm sure she knew something bizarre was happening, but I had no idea what it was either.

As the woman approached I saw she was wearing a very heavy brown sweater. It was early spring, and the temperature earlier that day had been unseasonably warm, which was why I was wearing a sleeveless blouse myself, and the baby was so lightly dressed. I was a bit surprised to see her wearing something that heavy and warm on what had been such a hot day. But the sudden plunge of the temperature made me think she was probably more comfortably dressed than I was at that moment.

She walked slowly but deliberately toward my home, and I assumed she would acknowledge me as she approached, especially with the two of us suddenly being the only ones around. I planned to ask her if this didn't seem very strange to her too. But when she got close enough for eye contact and to exchange comments, she completely ignored me. It was as if she didn't even see me standing there, just a few metres away from the sidewalk. She didn't pass by, though, as I had expected her to. She stopped when she got to the large maple tree growing on our boulevard and stared at it for several seconds with a look of rapture on her face ... and that unsettled me. But nothing prepared me for what she did next.

What I had thought was a heavy woollen sweater covering her arms and upper body was actually countless tent caterpillars. I finally realized this as I watched in horror as she slowly started to peel them, one after another, off of herself and place them onto the tree. I stood watching this for a few moments, completely shocked and frozen to the spot. I could not believe what I was seeing. Finally, my anger at her deliberate infestation of our lovely tree surpassed my bewilderment and fear of the strangeness of that whole experience.

I called to her from the porch, "Hey, stop that!"

She either ignored me or was unaware of my presence, because she never even turned to look in my direction. She just continued to peel off caterpillar after caterpillar from her upper body and place them gently onto the trunk of the tree.

"What are you doing?" I yelled again. This time she did acknowledge me. She turned and glared at me in the most terrifying way, and I almost fainted on the spot. I was prepared to just rush back into the house and let her strip every last caterpillar off of herself as she seemed intent on doing, rather than confront her again. But before I could move she backed away from the tree, still wearing hundreds of the caterpillars on her arms and body, and slowly retraced her path back down the street.

Twice she turned and glared at me again, but she finally reached the intersection and turned the corner out of sight. I felt weak with relief. And as quickly as the clouds had set in and the sun had disappeared, the day was bright and beautifully warm once more. And all the usual noises filled our street again within the split second it took me to leave the front porch and re-enter the living room to pick up my daughter from her playpen and hold her close. I was even relieved to hear the chainsaw in my neighbour's backyard again. I talked calmly and reassuringly to my baby, but I was shaking like a leaf.

After knowing she was all right, I put her in the playpen again and headed back out to the boulevard with a broom in my hand. I knocked as many caterpillars off of the tree as I could reach, but many more had already climbed too high into the tree's limbs. And, no wonder, we did have a terrible infestation of tent caterpillars in that tree that year. My husband knew that was true, because he was the one who dealt with that difficult situation along with his usual yardwork that summer; but I know he could never really comprehend this story I tried to explain regarding the cause. I don't know that I could have truly believed it either, though, if I hadn't experienced it myself.

Everything about it was so eerie and surreal. My daughter was too young to retain the memory, but at the time I was grateful for her company. Her wide-eyed amazement validated everything I also was experiencing that day. I know it wasn't a dream or hallucination, and really did happen just as I have described. I just don't understand why or how.

———

HAUNTED NEIGHBOUR

My neighbour's house was haunted. It was built on an empty lot, and the house had just been built when they moved into it when I was a teenager. Their son was my age, and we were friends.

He always preferred to be at my house instead of his, and at first I thought he liked the commotion of being in our large family's home filled with lots of people, unlike his quiet home where he was the only child.

But one day he told me that he was scared living in his house and wanted his parents to sell it and move, but they wouldn't. He even asked if he could go and live with his grandparents in another city because he hated it there so much, but they wouldn't let him do that either.

He told me he had seen and heard ghosts in his house, but his parents wouldn't believe him and got mad if he talked about it. I asked what he had seen, and he listed off a lot of things, but I remember these two the most. An old lady walked into his room one night when he was reading in bed and sat down in a nearby chair and smiled at him. He said he screamed and she disappeared and then his father yelled at him for scaring his mother. Another time a little girl was sitting on the floor in his kitchen when he got home from school. No one else was home. She looked at him for a couple of seconds and then vanished.

Looking back now, I wish I had realized and been more sympathetic to how badly this was affecting him; but I was just a kid too, and unfortunately was more fascinated than sympathetic. I thought it was great, like something out of the movies, and wanted to see these ghosts too. So I started suggested going to his place whenever we got together from then on.

It was a while longer before I saw anything there myself, though, and I was starting to wonder if he had been making it all up. But one time (the last time) I spent the night at his place we stayed up late watching TV. Finally, after he fell asleep and the TV was turned off, I lay there still wide awake and heard someone walking down the hall with heavy footsteps. At first I assumed it was one of his parents, because their room was across the hall from his. But I knew they had both gone to bed long before we did, and I hadn't heard anyone leave that room since. I could see from the space under the door that the hallway was still dark (I figured they would have turned on the hall light). And the footsteps came to his door, not theirs.

I could hear (and sense) someone on the other side of that door for quite a while. I was a pretty cocky teenager, but I'll admit now that scared me, and I wanted to wake up my friend, but kept straining my ears instead, hoping to hear the footsteps walking away. I could hear the muffled sounds of someone leaning or brushing against the door, and I can still remember how it made me feel lying in the dark, not knowing what I was hearing on the other side of that door.

Finally, I heard what sounded like muttering, and then the loud footsteps went back down the hall again.

I didn't sleep for the rest of that night. Next morning I told my friend what had happened. He just nodded his head and told me he had heard that same thing before too, many times.

To his relief his parents finally sold the house a few months later.

—————

NO MORE DENIAL

I admit I am currently living in a haunted house. I was in denial about that for a while when we bought this house last year. It's our first house. My wife and I have been married two years, and we thought it would be a great investment and get us onto the property ladder. It was priced right and didn't need too much work to be inhabitable. Mostly just some minor repairs and updates in the kitchen and bathroom and some coats of paint have turned it back into a nice-looking house. But how it looks and how it feels are different things.

The first thing I tried to ignore were the smells. Cigar smoke and very strong perfume seem to combine into a pungent odour that suddenly hits you in two areas of the house: the upstairs hallway and near the back door by the kitchen. I don't know why this is contained to only those areas, but it is.

Our two cats and boxer pup seem pretty nervous (skittish, as my wife would call it) in the house and are always following something with their eyes, unseen by us. They will focus on something about six feet above them and keep whatever it is in their sight as if it's travelling around the room. If it appears to come to close to the animals they will open their eyes wider in fright, and then race out of the room and go and hide somewhere. It's hard to describe how creepy this actually is, watching how the animals react to this. I just thought they were having a hard time adjusting to their new home at first, but this is still going on, and they should be used to it here by now, especially the pup who was bought after we moved into the house.

Once my wife let out a scream, and when I went downstairs to see what was wrong she told me she thought I had come up behind her and tickled her waist, but when she turned around no one was there. We both started to feel a bit less comfortable living here after that.

My car keys are always moved whenever I leave them near the front door. We have a table near the door, and I always toss the keys there out of habit when I enter the house. But they are never there when I go to leave again. Sometimes they are even upstairs or in the basement, areas I hadn't been to during that interval in the house. Once I purposely put them there and waited to see what would happen. Nothing. They were on that table all day, exactly where I'd put them. But when my wife came home and I greeted her at the door they were gone by the time I turned toward the table to show her they hadn't been moved.

I found them on the counter in the kitchen that time. No idea how they got there, but I stopped leaving them on the table after that and always keep them in my pocket now.

A few weeks ago I got home from work about an hour before my wife did and went into our bedroom to grab a shower and change my clothes because we were going out later that night. My wife and I had left the house together that morning. The door to our room is always kept closed to keep the pets out when we aren't there, and it was that day too. So I know they hadn't been in there. When I opened the door I saw a huge imprint on our bed where it looked like a large person had been lying on it.

We've stopped trying to make ourselves believe this is a normal household. We know it's haunted; we don't know why, though. It's not really that old. As far as we know nothing terrible ever happened here, and the original owner didn't die in the house; she just got too old to live alone and lives with her daughter now.

I don't think we'll be here long enough to solve the mystery of this haunting, if it even could be solved. We planned to stay for a few years when we bought it, but we hope to move a lot sooner than that now.

———

HOUSE-SITTING

Our neighbours were going on a holiday and asked me to house-sit for them while they were gone. This wasn't a problem, as I lived on the same street so could keep an eye on their property for them, water their plants, take in the mail, etc.

They had a beautiful old home, the nicest in the neighbourhood, if not the whole town. And I had never heard or seen anything unusual while visiting there before, and my friends certainly never mentioned anything to me about thinking their house was haunted. But the first time I was alone in the house, to water the plants while they were away, I started to get an uneasy feeling I never expected to have. When I came in I noticed the radio was on in the kitchen, which I thought was unusual since the house was empty, but I didn't think that much about it until I turned it off and then heard it playing again as I was looking for the watering can for the plants in another room.

And it felt like I was being watched, but I knew I was the only one in the house. I tried to ignore that uneasy feeling and went into the next room to water the plant in there. As I walked toward the large plant in the corner of the room, the chair beside it slid right across the floor about three feet toward me. I never watered the plant that day. I rushed out of there instead.

But they were gone for a month, and I had already promised to take care of the plants for them, so knew I would have to go back eventually. So I made my husband go with me the next time. He is the most skeptical person around, and didn't believe for a minute that a ghost had pushed that chair across the floor the last time I had been there. He had a few other explanations (my imagination, the house's old foundation made the floors uneven, a dog or cat could have pushed it — even though they didn't have any pets).

He went into the house first and had a quick look around and then motioned to me to come in. His back was to the staircase, and as he made smartass remarks about getting our friends a "Ghostbusters" gift certificate for Christmas that year something started to form behind him, over the stairs.

He saw my expression, and turned to see what I was looking at. And we both saw a vortex-like "thing" (I don't know what else to call it) suspended in mid-air. It just suddenly materialized, and then evaporated into nothing again within a few seconds. I was so glad he was witnessing this too.

I better not quote what he said when he saw it, but let's just say he isn't quite as skeptical about other people's paranormal sightings anymore.

A few days later I was unlocking their front door to place the mail on the pile on the front stand. Something caught my eye, and I thought I saw someone walking in the living room. I nervously peeked around the corner and screamed when I saw a woman standing there. It was my friend, home sooner than expected, and my reaction scared her too and she also screamed. She thought I had mistaken her for an intruder, but I actually screamed because I had thought she was a ghost. After we both stopped laughing I decided it might be best not to mention what we had seen. I had already scared her enough.

———

CENTRAL CANADA

HAUNTED CHILDHOOD

This took place in my childhood home, where I lived with my sister, mother, and father. The house was a typical 1960s-era side-split design, in a new neighbourhood that had previously just been farmland. It was nothing like the Victorian gothic mansions that are usually associated with restless spirits and hauntings.

We had never experienced any paranormal activity in our previous house, and certainly didn't expect it in our brand new one. And we never could understand why that particular house was so haunted.

After we moved in to the new house it was at least three or four years before anything unusual occurred. It all started on Remembrance Day one year when my sister and I were home, as it was a school holiday at that time, and our parents were both at work. We were sitting on the couch in the living room, arguing about something trivial. Suddenly, across the room, the television turned on all by itself, and the volume kept increasing until it was as loud as it could go. My sister and I looked at each other in shock and forgot about whatever had caused our squabble.

One afternoon soon after that, I returned home for lunch. I had been the last one to leave the house that morning, and knew everything had been quiet when I had closed and locked the door on my way to school. But now, when I stood on our front porch unlocking the door a few hours later, I could hear music blaring from inside the house. It was so loud the windows were actually shaking and our dog was frantically running around, trying to escape the noise.

When I got the door opened I ran into the dining room and saw that a Christmas album was playing on the record player in there, with the volume turned up to maximum. I knew the house had been silent when I left for school that morning, and no one had been using the record player for several days prior to that. But now, when the house had been unoccupied since I had left after breakfast, the record player had somehow been turned on, with the volume fully cranked. Our dog was relieved when I turned off the music, but it took a while before she stopped shaking.

It then became a fairly common occurrence to hear music playing within the house. Sometimes it would be audible but faint, and walking around the house would not help in determining where the noise was originating.

Conversations between at least two people, and sometimes what sounded like several, could be heard as faint murmuring too; and this, even more than the music, confused and frightened us. The voices would continue until we entered the room where they seemed to be, and then they would abruptly stop until we left the room again.

My sister and I seemed to observe the most activity, although on one occasion our mother nervously admitted she had seen a young man with a guitar slung over his shoulder walk down the hallway and stop at her bedroom door. He looked in the room to where she was lying in bed, reading a book. They stared at one another for several seconds and then he just simply vanished.

We were surprised to hear our mother share this experience, and to see how frightened she was, because she had not seemed to believe our own claims up until that point. After that, though, she did not so easily shrug off our constant stories of doors opening by themselves and appliances (the television, and radio, etc.) being turned on and off by unseen hands.

Although the haunting was really frightening at times, nothing harmful ever happened. The ghosts definitely made their presence known, but not in aggressive ways.

One day, though, my sister and I were sitting on the bed talking in her bedroom when, from several feet away, a small rubber Super Ball suddenly shot up off of the dresser (neither of us had been near it or touched it). With incredible force it bounced itself off of every wall in the room and whizzed by our heads. We ran screaming from the bedroom. And as soon as we left the room, the ball stopped, and it was sitting still, on the dresser again, when we felt brave enough to return. That incident definitely scared us the most.

Ten years after our family moved into that house, my mother died suddenly after a brief illness. The paranormal activity in the house, which had occurred so frequently up until then, completely stopped from that day on. And although we remained in the house for several more years after that, I can't recall there being another single incident.

Maybe my mother's spirit was protectively watching over us and wouldn't let other spirits bother us anymore.

The House Beside the Mill

My experience is very much remembered through the eyes of a child, as I was only about eleven or twelve for the bulk of the time that I lived in this house. My family, particularly my aunt, who owned the house, would provide a far more insightful articulation of this story, but I doubt it is a story she would care to retell. The experiences in this house were not at all pleasant and were the impetus for her to relocate her family to another home.

My aunt was puzzled by the high vacancy rate of the house and the surprisingly low lease payments that were being asked by the owner, who was trying to sell it. She was, however, ecstatic about the find and gratefully signed the lease and moved her family in.

The house was located in a small town (population around three thousand), at the end of a small dead-end street beside a mill that had burnt down sometime at the turn of the twentieth century and been rebuilt.

The house itself was beautiful. It was built in the colonial style and was two stories, with white wood siding and four ominous (but stately) dormers across the front. Upstairs, there was a master bedroom, a regular bedroom, and a third bedroom that had a small room off of it. At one time it must have served as the quarters for a nanny or wet nurse. The main floor contained a kitchen, dining room, living room, and drawing room. The floors were connected by a grand spiral staircase.

One of the strangest features of the house was the basement, which contained many antiques and treasures that must have come with the original house and that, surprisingly, no one had taken. There was a door down there that led out, underground, to a tunnel connecting to a smaller house on the street behind. This, apparently, was the tunnel that connected the main house to what was perhaps the servants' quarters behind it. While the house was by no means a mansion, it was somewhat strange and out of place in comparison to the other houses in this small town.

I lived in this house for two months one summer, when my parents shipped me off for summer vacation, and I spent many weekends here as well. I can't quite recall how long my aunt actually lived there, but I don't think it was much longer than a year.

I realized very quickly that there was something unusual about this house. The day my aunt moved in I was around to help unpack the boxes, and I remember feeling a weight in the house that was unsettling. It's hard to know if this was a child's intuition or simply the discomfort that comes with being in an unfamiliar place, but it was there nonetheless.

The darkest and most unsettling room was the bedroom on the second floor that served as the nanny's room. It is hard to describe, but it was a cold and damp and heavy-feeling room, quite unlike any of the other rooms. For the duration of the time that my aunt lived there, it remained very unused. It served as a guest bedroom that everyone refused to sleep in, though no one ever really articulated why.

My aunt's two-year-old son slept in the small room off the nanny's quarters, and her baby daughter slept in the master bedroom with her parents. The other bedroom was also a guest room, and my room when I stayed for the summer.

The first occurrences in the house revolved around the sound of a child crying. In the first instance this was not unusual, as my aunt had two small children. But when she went to check on them she would find her children fast asleep or playing peacefully with no sign of being distressed. Later, we would get used to hearing the sound of a child on the stairs, sliding down on their behind, one [step] at a time, and laughing.

There was also the constant sound of someone pacing in the hallway, back and forth, for hours on end. Only when we climbed up the stairs to see who was there would the pacing stop. There were days where we would hole up in the kitchen, with the pacing overhead, clinging to the hope that whoever, or whatever, was up there would not come down the stairs and show themselves.

My aunt's young son seemed most tuned into the presence, and would often blurt out, "Who's that man?" He would point to the corner shadows of the room where no man was ever seen standing. Some nights he would wake up screaming, obviously afraid, and would refuse to return to his small room to sleep. Near the end of my aunt's stay at the house, everyone crammed into the master bedroom to sleep.

Doors slammed, household items disappeared and reappeared, floor and walls shook, and voices were heard whispering as everyday occurrences. An old bureau in the bedroom where I slept held a mirror that, if you pulled it away from the wall, could be flipped around. (I am not sure if you are familiar with this particular piece of furniture, but it is fairly common. There was a mirror on the front side and wood on the back side, and it was built to accommodate all the various superstitions around mirrors.) Often, I would leave the room only to return to find the mirror had been flipped around (an impossibility considering the piece of furniture was extremely heavy and the mirror could only be flipped when it was pulled clear from the wall).

My aunt had a number of psychics and clairvoyants through the house and tried an endless number of things to rid the house of the ghosts. She tried to hold seances, she put salt in all of the corners to "absorb" the energy, she lit candles, she prayed, and on and on and on. All to no avail.

Strangers who came to investigate the haunting would leave the house after poking around (particularly in the basement), and almost all of them met with some bizarre accident or illness upon leaving: car accidents, broken bones, strange illnesses, etc.

The last day I slept in the house, before returning to my parents' house, I was carrying my suitcase from my room upstairs to the front hall on the main floor. As I was descending the stairs, I felt a weight behind me, and I found myself lying at the bottom of the stairs with an incredible pain in my back. I pretended I was fine and waited for my dad on the front steps to pick me up. I remember irrationally thinking that if I told my aunt about the pain she would take me to the hospital and somehow I would be forced to recover from the fall in her house, as opposed to going home. This was an unfathomable thought for me, after living two months on edge. I remember getting home and crying for days (and finding out three years later that I had a slipped disc in my back from the fall).

After that summer, I think my aunt stayed for a few more months before moving out. My uncle, who refused to believe that there was such a thing as a ghost, came home one night and saw the ghostly image of a man standing in the drawing room. Wasting no time, he grabbed a hunting rifle and shot at it, leaving a bullet hole in the wall and scaring the life out of my aunt and his kids. This was the last straw. The next day my aunt moved out.

My aunt did a lot of research into the history of the house, including the fire that destroyed the mill next to it. She still believes that the sounds of the children crying and playing have something to do with the child labourers who died in the mill fire.

SOMEONE TO WATCH OVER ME

I grew up in a very volatile environment due to my parents' alcoholism. One night when I was pretty young my mother and father had a particularly horrible fight, and I was terrified.

After everything calmed down and everyone else was sleeping that night, I was still lying in bed, wide awake, frightened and crying. There was a night light on in the room. At one point in the night I remember a strong feeling that someone was watching me, so I looked up from my pillow and saw an enormous shadow filling two walls: the wall beside the bed that I was on, and on the other wall, right behind the bed. It looked like a huge shadow of a nun's head and shoulders. We weren't Catholic, and I hadn't been praying, just crying. It wasn't any religious influence that would have made me think that, but I could immediately see that is what it seemed to be.

From the position of the shadow, it looked like she was right above me and looking down protectively, and that gave me immediate comfort. And I felt so much better when I saw this. I stopped crying and just stared at the shadow for a long time, and was so glad it was there with me.

Finally, though, I began to get curious as to what was actually casting the shadow. I got out of bed and looked around the night light and the rest of the room to see what could be creating it. But there was nothing that seemed to be causing it. Yet there it was, right above my bed, and so clearly defined. And I knew it had not been there for the first few hours I was in bed, it just suddenly appeared.

I climbed back into bed, exhausted, but kept opening my eyes to make sure the shadow was still there. It stayed above me all night. I finally fell asleep, and when I woke up in the early morning, the shadow was gone. I never saw it again. But I have never forgotten that, and I think it must have been a protective spirit, or angel, letting me know she was watching over me.

_____

Do You See What I See?

I was helping my friend move into an apartment. After unpacking all of the boxes and getting everything organized, we went into the living room to take a break. The living room was situated at the end of the hall that led to the bathroom and bedroom.

While leaning against a wall in the living room I could see out of the corner of my eye that someone was approaching us from the hall. I turned and saw a middle-aged brunette woman in a navy blue dress walking up the hall toward the living room. She stared straight at me, and our eyes met for a second. She didn't look very happy to see me standing there. Then she slowly turned around and headed back down the hall toward the bedroom.

My friend was also looking toward the hall in a curious way, and asked if I'd just heard someone walk toward us, stop, and then walk back down the hall again.

I explained that I had just seen that woman, but had not heard any footsteps. So we both thought that was really strange; I had clearly seen an apparition, or whatever it was, of a woman but hadn't heard any sound. My friend had clearly heard the sound of footsteps walking toward us and then away again, but did not see anything at all.

We did a thorough check of the hall/bedroom/bathroom area, of course, but no one was there. We were the only two people in that apartment.

OUIJA

When I was growing up my family had a Ouija board, and sometimes we would play with it. I never felt comfortable with the idea of communicating with spirits, though, so I never directly participated. But I was always curious enough to want to see what would happen when others used it.

My cousins were using the board one day. One of my cousins and I have the same unique name (and the same unusual spelling). So when the two people using the board asked who the next message was for, my name (and my cousin's name) was spelled out. I was about twelve years old at the time. We asked which person they meant, and then my last name was also spelled, so it was clear the message was intended for me and not my cousin who had a different last name.

I was uncomfortable by the whole idea of a Ouija board and sure didn't want to be singled out for any specific message from it. I asked my cousins to put it away, but they said they wanted to see the message and went ahead using it. The message was that I was going to die when I was thirty. Even though thirty sounded pretty old when I was only twelve, I was still upset about that message. If anyone else had been using the board I may have suspected they were just trying to frighten me and made that message appear themselves. But I could tell my cousins were almost as disturbed by what was spelled out as I was, and I knew they hadn't caused it to spell that.

When I asked, with forced bravery, how my death was supposed to occur the word *cancer* was spelled out.

I asked my cousins to put the board away, and that time they listened to me, and we never used it again when they came to our house. And although I tried to tell myself it was just a silly game that couldn't possibly have the ability to predict the future, I still couldn't help but think about that message occasionally as my thirtieth birthday approached. But fortunately quite a few years have come and gone since that age and the message was proven to be false.

My next, and last, experience with a Ouija board was after graduating from college, when I shared a house with a few roommates. One day two of us were out shopping and happened to pass by a thrift shop. We saw an old Ouija board was for sale in the window, so thought it might be fun to buy it. We were having a get-together with some friends that night and thought it would be funny to play with that. I didn't expect to have a repeat of my last experience on that other board from my childhood, and thought it would just be entertaining, if it even worked at all.

The board we bought was old, and it didn't have the planchette with it in the box still, so to improvise we used an upside-down glass. Two girls at the party put their fingers on the base of the glass, and we all proceeded to shout out questions about our careers, love lives, etc. Nothing happened at first, and we thought it wasn't going to work. Then, just as we suggested giving up and putting the board away, the glass tipped over. The two girls using the board jumped, because neither of them even had their fingers on it at the time.

One of them then asked, "Is anyone there who would like to speak to us?"

The glass immediately moved to the YES on the board and kept sliding back and forth across the word in a very strong movement.

At first it seemed as though the two girls had to be moving the glass themselves, because how else could it slide around like that? But the more questions that were asked the quicker the response seemed to be, and at times the girls were barely able to even keep their fingers connected to the glass because it was moving around the board so fast, spelling out the responses.

The answers to the questions were very innocent at first. But after a while the tone (maybe *intent* is a better word to use) seemed to change, and the answers became nasty and sounded angry.

One of our friends couldn't be there that night because she had to work a very early shift at work the next morning so she was at home in bed. Nevertheless, after a few more minutes, no matter what questions were asked, the message kept only spelling out that our friend wasn't there with us that night. We all thought it was strange that it kept doing that but didn't worry about it too much at first. But then it started spelling out how our friend was soon going to be murdered. It gave the exact time, day, and month this would happen and described it graphically.

I got angry and told the two girls that they shouldn't even joke about something horrible like that. They insisted they weren't doing it, and one got up and asked if I wanted to try it for myself to see that the glass really was moving on its own.

By that point I was getting a little nervous of the board and really didn't want to get too close to it, but I didn't want those kinds of messages to continue and really thought once I had my fingers on the glass I would make that stop.

When I put my fingers on the glass I was barely touching it, and I could see the other girl was just lightly resting her fingers against it too. But no sooner had I sat down and touched the glass than it began to slide quickly around the board spelling out more gruesome messages. I knew I wasn't making it do that, and I could tell the other girl wasn't either because she even had a hard time keeping her fingers on the glass at all because it was moving so quickly.

We got so scared from the messages it was spelling out about our friend that someone telephoned her to see if she was all right. (I'm sure she didn't appreciate having us wake up her that late, when she was asleep.)

When we all expressed how relieved we were that she was safe and sound at home the board again spelled out the specific time and date this murder was predicted to occur in the near future. It was so scary.

The glass then tipped over again by itself. When we put it back in place the other girl using the board asked if anyone else was there who wanted to talk to us.

This time the glass began to spell out words in a much more gentle and slower manner. It said it was her father spelling out the messages now. He had died several years previously.

The words being spelled out over and over were: "Stop using this now ... it is not a game ... stop using this now ... it is not a game ..."

There was some giggling in the crowd, and the glass began to move quicker and with more force as though in response to the laughter, and repeated the message: "Stop using this right now ... it is not a game ..."

The two of us using the board decided that was good advice, and not only did we not want to use it anymore, we didn't even want to keep it in our house. So we put it into a big paper bag and went together to the side of the townhouse complex where there was a large, empty Dumpster. We threw the bag into the garbage and ran back into the house, relieved to be rid of it.

The next morning my roommate yelled to me to come quickly, and I ran downstairs to see what was wrong. I looked outside and could see the bag was now back at our front door. My friend thought the board had crawled back to us!

It had been a windy night, and obviously the bag had just been blown out of the Dumpster and landed back at our front door. But after looking into the Dumpster and then around the property we never could find the board again, so we weren't sure whatever happened to it. We all had a good laugh at our friend thinking it had "crawled back," though, and teased her about watching too many horror movies.

But, regardless of whatever happened to that Ouija board, I will always remember that experience. Our friend is still alive and well, and the gruesome prediction of her murder proved false when the date the board had spelled out came and went without incident, thank goodness.

I really think Ouija boards can be sinister. If my cousins didn't purposefully spell out that message about my death just to scare me, and I am sure they did not, then why would it spell out a thing like that? I don't know what it is that makes those things actually work the way they do, but if it is spirits communicating, it makes me wonder what kind of evil spirit would want to frighten a twelve-year-old like that. And obviously that message about our friend's murder was spelled out just to terrify us too, which it certainly did.

———

OUT-OF-BODY EXPERIENCES

My experiences aren't about being haunted, but are about a spirit. My own, and how it has left my body twice during near-death experiences.

I grew up in a very large family, and am the third youngest of ten. My father died when I was only five.

Not long after his death I got measles. I had pneumonia too, and was very sick.

I was lying on the chesterfield downstairs in the living room, feeling so ill and scared, because I saw how frightened my mother was when the doctor examined me and then asked her to step into the hallway with him to talk. I could hear her crying, and I remember closing my eyes and starting to cry too.

Suddenly I felt completely better in every way. I opened my eyes in relief, but immediately realized that something very astonishing was happening. I was floating up at the ceiling and looking down at myself still lying on the chesterfield below. I wasn't frightened being up so high, although I have been terrified of heights all my life. I stared down at myself, thinking how small and sad I looked, when I heard my mother crying again out in the hallway with the doctor. As soon as I heard her, I wanted to be with her, and as soon as I thought that, I was then immediately in the hallway with her, still floating up at the ceiling, but now looking down at my mother and the doctor where they stood by the front door.

He kept saying to keep me as comfortable as possible, and that he was very sorry. I knew he was trying to comfort my mother, and I knew it was because she was so sad about me. But I felt so good now, and I wanted her to know I wasn't sick anymore.

As soon as I thought that, I was back in my body, lying on the chesterfield, and then feeling so badly again.

But my fever broke, and my mother said it was a miracle that I survived. I was told it must have been a dream when I tried to explain about floating out of my body the way I had. But when I was able to tell my mother, verbatim, what she and the doctor had said to each other, she realized I could have only known that if I'd been in the hallway with them because they spoke in whispered tones of my serious illness, and it would have been impossible for me to have known exactly what was said from where I lay in the other room behind closed doors.

I know my spirit briefly left my body as I had that near-death experience.

Many years later when I was married and had just had my third baby, the delivery was very difficult and I had almost not survived it. When I was finally out of the hospital and back at home recuperating, but still bedridden, my mother was staying with us, caring for the two older children and the new baby.

One day, as I lay in bed, I started to feel very strange. I called out, but no one came, and I realized I was alone in the house, and I was sure I was dying and wanted my mother with me.

The shades were pulled down in the room so it had been dark, but suddenly it was almost blindingly bright, and at first I wondered what happened to the wall in my bedroom because now I was looking right into the backyard. But then I realized I was actually outside myself, and no longer in my bed. And, again, I was floating.

It was a gorgeous sunny day, and I could see my two older children playing on the swing set in the yard, the baby was in his carriage, and my mother was leaning on the fence as she talked to our next door neighbour.

And, as with my mother and the doctor when I was young, I could hear their entire conversation about how worried everyone was that I was still so weak. But I felt incredible, not sick at all anymore. And just as I was feeling so lucky to feel so well again, I was suddenly back in my body, in bed, in that darkened room. And I quickly recovered after that.

Definitely Not Welcomed

We lived in a haunted house for over ten years, and for the most part it was easy to coexist with the ghost. Knocking on walls and the smell of freshly baked bread were the most common occurrences. Sometimes our shoes would go missing for days and then show up again right at the door where they'd been last seen. Our dog would get very agitated and often stare at something near the ceiling and whine. But all in all it was never anything too unusual, and never threatening in any way.

Then came the night of our daughter's first date. When she invited Stan into our home, we all met him and thought he seemed like a nice kid. As she led him down the hallway and into the family room at the back of the house I could hear a series of loud crashes and went to see what was going on.

By the time I got to the family room too, I saw what had caused all that racket. A family portrait (of ancestors from over a hundred years ago) had somehow flown down the hallway and smashed on the floor right where Stan was standing in the doorway of the family room. And another very old picture (of a great-uncle from that same family as in the other portrait), in a very heavy brass frame, had smashed on the wall right beside the boy's head as he started to enter the room. This photo had been on the windowsill on the opposite side of the room. No one had been anywhere near either of these photos.

I only heard the noise, but my daughter and her date saw them actually flying through the air right at him. My daughter was shaking, but poor Stan was too shocked to even move.

After cleaning up the glass from the shattered frames, I reassured the kids it was just a freak accident and not to worry about it (but wasn't so reassured myself).

They dated for several months, and the longer we knew him the more we all started to realize Stan was not such a nice kid as we had once thought. He was a good actor, though, and it took a while before his true character was known. But the moment he walked into our house, something or someone was very protective of our daughter, or just hated him, and definitely didn't want him there.

I don't think there was a time during the length of their relationship that something didn't hit or trip him while he was in our house. He constantly said it felt like someone was trying to push him down the stairs (and succeeded many times). And one particularly scary incident was the time he went into the kitchen to get a snack and a large butcher knife fell (flew?) off a counter on the other side of the room and landed on his foot with enough force that the blade impaled the top of his foot, right through his shoe, and he received a deep cut.

No one else was ever subjected to any kind of abuse when we lived there. But Stan couldn't walk into the house without something falling off a wall or flying across the room right at him. It would actually have been fascinating if it wasn't always so startling and violent.

After that relationship ended, nothing like that ever happened to anyone else ever again. The ghost treated him (and only him) like that.

Eastern Canada

Cottage Life

We once bought an old cottage that had belonged to an elderly man and woman for about fifty years, but when the husband died, the wife never used it again and so it was vacant for a while before we got it.

When we purchased the cottage, all the furniture and contents were included, so the only thing about it that changed was the ownership. After listening to some of the nearby neighbours' stories about the old man who had owned it, it was clear how much he had loved it there. We knew that before he died, he and his wife and their dog had spent a lot of time up there, and their grown children and grandchildren often visited too.

The first summer we were there we were all playing cards around the kitchen table one night when our oldest daughter jumped about a foot in her chair. She said a medium-sized white dog had just rushed past the table and out the kitchen door into the living room. No one else had noticed anything, but she was so positive of what she had seen, and so flustered, we all got up to search for the strange animal. But we couldn't find the dog anywhere.

We might have been inclined to think she had just imagined the whole thing, but a while after that, my husband and I saw this dog too. It suddenly appeared as though it had run right through the cottage wall from the outside. Like it was chasing something or someone at top

49

speed. Then it either just disappeared or went right through another wall back to the outside again. It all happened so fast it was almost just a blur of white. This was more amazing than frightening, though, and I was glad my husband was with me to see it too.

Our son woke up one night and cried out for us, saying someone was standing near his bed. By the time we got to his room whoever it was had gone, but that left him feeling pretty frightened.

We also all saw an old man walking around the exterior of the cottage on a number of occasions. A few times we would hurry out of the cottage to see who it was when we saw him looking in at us through one of the windows, but once we got outside there was never a trace of him. It would have been really difficult for someone to run away from that cottage without being seen or heard.

Once after seeing him outside we heard a knock on the door. This did frighten our daughter a bit, so she called out and asked who it was. He replied that he wanted to talk to her mother, but by the time I opened the door he had again vanished and we never saw him again after that.

THE MAILROOM GHOST

During my first year of college I worked part-time in the residence mailroom on the campus, and being before the days of e-mail, my shifts were very busy sorting all those students' letters. I hardly had time to look up from the piles of mail I had to distribute into the alphabetically arranged compartments.

My shifts were usually late at night, and no one else was ever around. The only sounds were the ticking of the clock and the rustling of the envelopes as I sifted through the endless piles. The radio would never work in that area for some reason, and I usually just left it off instead of having to constantly tune it, trying to pick up a signal.

One night I was working alone as usual, but had a very uncomfortable feeling. This was not normal for me, as I had never been bothered by the solitude of that job before. But on this night I could not shake the feeling I was being watched. Every time I looked up from my work

I expected to see someone standing there because the feeling was so strong, I assumed someone was there.

The radio was not turned on. I had tried to get a station to come in at the start of my shift and had given up and shut it off because I hated the static. As I sat with my back to the open door in the mailroom, trying to resist the urge to constantly turn around, it finally got too strong, and I couldn't keep myself from turning to look again to see if anyone was there.

And that time there was. A young man, in his early twenties I would say, was leaning against the doorjamb looking at me as I sat at the desk across the room. I wasn't sure if he was actually staring at me or just daydreaming in my direction, because it seemed to take a minute before he realized I was looking at him. When our eyes connected it seemed to startle him as much as it did me (maybe even more); and just as I saw him jump a bit, the radio on the desk suddenly turned on. That really startled me.

When the radio came on, he took a step backwards from where he was leaning and then seemed to freeze, as though he couldn't decide if he should leave or stay. But all the time our eyes were locked, and I thought he was going to say something to me.

Now normally back then, being a young woman alone in that isolated mailroom late at night, just having a strange man show up out of nowhere would have been enough to alarm me. I always made sure the main door leading to that area was locked behind me when I came in for my shift, and the door to the mailroom itself would have been inaccessible to anyone without a key to the main door beyond it. But neither of those facts occurred to me in that moment.

I didn't feel threatened, though, but he definitely seemed nervous of me, or at least of being seen standing there. And just as I wondered why he wasn't saying anything, he slowly started to disappear. He slowly faded into nothing. I was left staring at empty space, but could still feel his presence there. It was the oddest experience I have ever had. And even at the time I wondered why I wasn't more afraid of what I was seeing.

I sat very still for a few moments and decided to leave early that night, because I didn't want to stay there alone any longer. But I didn't go screaming out of there. I packed up my things, with a feeling like I was moving in slow motion, and locked up. I kept looking all around me, still feeling like he was nearby. Even on the quick walk back to my dorm room it seemed like he was walking along beside me.

The next day I had to return to the mailroom to pick up a textbook I had forgotten the night before, and saw one of the daytime staff there. She was a middle-aged woman, and had always just ignored me any time she saw me before.

But on this day she was friendly to me and even called me by name, which surprised me because I didn't think she even knew what it was. She asked if I enjoyed working the part-time night shift, and winked when she asked if the "ghost" bothered me at all.

Her wink made it seem like she was joking, but I still felt myself tense a bit when she said that. I just smiled, though, and told her I didn't believe in ghosts (I didn't want to talk about my experience with her). But she surprised me by telling me that she was a firm believer now. She told me it was haunted in that office, and then she told me why.

About twenty years ago, a group of boys were walking outside of that building and two of them got into an argument that led to a fight. They ended up inside somehow, possibly one was trying to get away from the other, but the one boy fell, or was pushed, and hit his head against a pipe by the main door. He died instantly. It was such a senseless tragedy. A young guy's life cut so short like that. I shuddered at her story, thinking of him dying right there.

She told me everyone who worked there, including herself, had seen his ghost. I asked for a description without admitting I had also seen him just the previous night. She described him exactly, even the birthmark on his left cheek. But I still didn't want to talk to her about my own experience. She treated the haunting almost as a joke, like it amused her somehow. Maybe that was just nervous tension on her part.

But to me, it was so sad that he lost his life like that, and his spirit still remained at the scene all those years later.

I don't know if the mailroom employees are still seeing him to this day. I hope not. I hope he is finally at peace by now.

———

My Grandmother's Spirit

This isn't really about a place being haunted so much as an experience I had with a ghost. And since it was my grandmother, I prefer to call her a spirit.

When I was nine, my parents signed me up for a week away at a summer camp with our church. I didn't want to go. I had never been away from home before even for one night, never mind a whole week. I begged my parents not to make me go, but they kept telling me it was for the best.

I knew something was going on because my mother was so sad and there were a lot of long-distance phone calls from far-away relatives, which usually only happened on birthdays or Christmas. My parents seemed to want to get me out of the house, and that made me feel even worse and want to leave even less.

When I asked to see my grandmother before I left, and was told I couldn't, I really broke down. My grandmother and I were very close. I thought she would talk my mother into letting me stay home if I could just explain to her how scared I was to go. But no one would let me visit her, or even talk to her on the phone. So I felt completely miserable by the time I was put on the bus for camp at our church the next week.

I refused to admit it in the letter I wrote home, but I did enjoy myself there after the first few hours of feeling sorry for myself. The last night that I was at camp I was lying in my bottom bunk with my eyes closed, but I wasn't sleeping or dreaming. I felt the bunk sink down as someone sat beside me. And when I looked up, there was my grandmother, smiling down at me. She gently brushed the hair back from my eyes and cupped my cheeks in her hand, as she always did.

Looking back now it is surprising to me that I only felt comforted and excited to see her. I never wondered how she got there or why she had come alone, so late at night, to see me. I was just glad she was there. She sat there on my bunk holding my hand until I fell asleep.

My parents arrived to take me home the next morning, and I was eager to see them, but my mother looked even sadder than before I left. When we got to the car my father told me that my grandmother had died the night before. She had been very sick and dying in the hospital when I left for camp; that is why I couldn't see or phone her. My parents thought it would be best for me not to be there during that time, and that is why I was sent to camp that week.

I thought they were obviously mistaken and excitedly told them that my grandmother had come to see me the night before. I could see the glances they gave each other, and no one spoke for a while.

Finally my mother asked me how her mother had looked when I saw her. I told her she looked really happy. My mother cried a lot when I told her that, but said it made her feel so much better.

———

BAD VIBRATIONS

We like to take Sunday drives in the country and would often pass a quaint turn-of-the-century farmhouse that sits on top of a hill along a rural road just outside of town. I always thought it was abandoned. It wasn't boarded up, but there was never a vehicle or person anywhere around.

And I could never understand why it was not being lived in; I always enjoyed looking at it whenever our drives took us in that direction. So one day when we noticed a "For Sale" sign on the front lawn and another sign at the base of the long driveway indicating there was an open house that afternoon, I was curious to have a better look at it.

My husband wanted to see it too, so we pulled over to the side of the road and parked the car. As we walked toward the house, I realized for the first time what a fair distance the house was from the road, and as we got closer I started to get the weirdest feeling. I almost felt sick, I was feeling so anxious. I felt so stressed I just wanted to leave before we even entered the house, but had no idea why. I had felt fine in the car. That feeling just came out of nowhere and hit me so hard.

There were a few other couples wandering around the house and grounds. Every room had been freshly painted, and the floors had all been redone. But I couldn't shake that awful feeling, no matter how nice it looked. My husband was more interested in the plumbing and electrical service, though, and said he didn't have that same creepy feeling that I did.

It was a pretty good price, and the real estate agent said the vendors were motivated to sell. There was no furniture in the house, and even though recent work had been done on it, no one had actually lived there for a very long time.

The agent hosting the open house told us that a couple from the city had purchased it as a weekend country retreat, but the wife refused to ever live there. So the husband finally gave up trying to convince her to and decided to sell if they were never going to use it.

I thought I understood exactly why she didn't want to ever use it, if it gave her the same feeling I had. I wouldn't want go there either. It felt like a mixture of fear and grief, and it was so strong it made me wonder if there had been a gruesome murder there at some point, maybe even a hundred years ago, and that energy still haunted the property. Being from a quiet area like that, though, I thought I would have heard something at some time about an old crime like that, and had to assume that couldn't have been the case.

But I did learn some interesting history when we went to the back of the property to look over the rest of the grounds. We met another couple out there, and the husband (probably in his eighties now) told us he had grown up on a farm in that area. He said that years ago there had been a slaughterhouse on the bordering property. It was just an empty field now, but he said as a boy he had to help his father and brothers take their pigs there to be slaughtered.

As he told us about that, I wondered if those strong feelings of fear and sadness that seemed to hang over that property like a black cloud could have been the residual energy of all those helpless and scared animals being killed like that so close by.

I never mentioned the negative atmosphere I noticed to these strangers, but I had already told my husband how it made me feel, and he gave me a curious look as we heard about that possible connection.

If hauntings are possible due to the energy or spirit of a person, it must happen with animals too. And, as with people, if the animal's death was frightening and confusing, that could account for the restless spirit or lasting negative energy that could haunt the place where they died as well.

Before then I had thought of ghosts and hauntings as strictly a human phenomenon. But it only makes sense [that] if it applies to one kind of living being, it must apply to all living beings.

We never bought that country property, obviously. I'm not sure if anyone did. The "For Sale" sign is long gone, but the property still looks abandoned.

I mentioned this experience to a close friend recently, and she told me her sister had a very similar thing happen. She and her family bought a country property that had also sat vacant for a long time. My friend said her sister agreed to buy it because her husband wanted to retire there one day, and the small barn would be perfect for the workshop he had always wanted for woodworking projects.

She never felt comfortable in the house, but would almost be sick from the knot in the pit of her stomach every time she went into the barn. She even had a few panic attacks, which was something she had never had before in her life. It got to the point where she stopped going to the property on the weekends with her husband, and eventually they had to sell because it was causing such a problem in their marriage.

When it was put on the market, a neighbour finally told them that before they bought that property it had been a well-known fact in the community that a puppy mill had been operating out of that barn for years until the former owner's death. Many complaints had been made, but nothing was ever officially done to shut it down. But the sister and her husband had no idea that so many helpless animals had suffered there like that. And when she did learn about it, she thought that was probably the source of her own severe anxiety every time she went into that barn.

———

WORDS ON A WALL

We bought an old townhouse as an investment property. It was built in the 1870s and needed a lot of attention, so it was a work in progress for a long time. I liked working on it, though. It had the feel of a loving home, even when it was under reconstruction. But when I was there alone, I often thought I saw someone out of the corner of my eye. And there was always a strong presence on the upper stairway landing. Just as you reached the top of the stairs, it would feel as though someone was there waiting for you. But not in a scary way: more protective than anything.

The job I hated the most was peeling off the layers of wallpaper. But in one room, this turned out to be more like finding a time capsule.

As I peeled away all the layers of wallpaper, I eventually came to writing on the bare wall that had been there for decades.

The messages were written by the mother and daughter of the house at that time, and were funny, sweet, happy, and sad. They wrote of knowing their words would soon be covered with their new wallpaper, and of missing the father/husband who was away in the war. At first I thought of the Second World War, but realized after seeing dates on some of the messages that it was actually written during the First World War.

Afterwards I did some research, online and locally, to find out a bit more about the family who wrote those messages.

The woman was a seamstress, and she and her daughter were living there. The wife commented on hoping she'd have the decorating finished by the time her husband returned (referring, in part, to the new wallpaper she planned to cover those words with, I guess). Among many others, the daughter wrote messages about hoping her father would be home by Christmas. It was very bittersweet reading those words.

During my investigation I discovered that her father did come home safely from the war, but sadly, her mother died of heart failure, at home, just days before Christmas that same year. How sad that poor little girl must have been. All that time so worried about losing her father, only then to lose her mother so unexpectedly. The sadness of that thought haunted me more than anything else.

Not long afterwards, while we were working on the house, a couple showed up one day, and the woman asked if we minded if she had a look around because her grandmother had owned the house when she was a little girl and she wanted to see it again. We didn't mind at all and were happy to show them all the work we were doing to fix up her grandmother's old house.

She told me her grandmother had lived there during the 1960s and early 1970s, and she remembered everything being decorated in orange and lime green back then, and still shuddered at the memory. We both laughed at that.

Her husband asked her if she thought she should tell me about the ghost. His wife blushed a bit. She said I might think she was crazy, but she was sure the house was haunted when she stayed there as a young girl.

I was curious why she had felt that. She told me that she had seen a lady walking along the hall outside of her bedroom one night, and she could smell her perfume in her room sometimes, so she was sure she came in there sometimes too. Her grandmother never wore perfume because she was allergic to it, and she was much taller than the woman she saw in the hall. So she was sure it was not her grandmother she had seen and smelled.

I told her I believed her, and I did. I also sensed her there, and thought it was probably the same woman who had written on that wall while awaiting her soldier's return.

———

A HELPING HAND

I lived in this house with my family from the time I was two until I went away to university when I was eighteen, at which time my parents bought a new house.

I can't remember a time not being aware of the fact our house was haunted. Even though we were so young when we first moved there, my siblings and I almost immediately knew there was something strange about our new house. I loved living there, but I was also constantly scared when I was younger. It was never something I took for granted or could ignore.

Our house was over a century old and authentically restored. It actually felt like being back in the Victorian era when you were inside of our house. I'm not sure if that was due to my mother's decorating or just the atmosphere of the house itself, but everyone would always comment on that whenever they visited.

Our house was always kept pretty spotless, so when small handprints started to appear all over the walls in my bedroom my mother would wash them off and tell me I needed to clean my hands more often if I was leaving smudges all over like that. But it wasn't me. I could see those handprints appear, and they weren't from my hands. Sometimes, as I would point out to my mother, they would be so far up on the wall there would be no way I could even reach up that high.

Eventually they started to appear in other parts of the house too, but the main concentration was always my room.

In a house with three small children, handprints aren't unusual, of course … but these were unique. They were often much higher than any of us could reach, and often they would be more like scratches right into the plaster of the walls than just prints on the painted surface.

I noticed how bizarre this really was as I packed to go away to school and we were getting ready to sell the house. When I took down all of my posters and the walls were bare, you could see all of the small handprints covering the entire room, from floor to ceiling. I hadn't realized how many there were until then. And my room had been painted a few times since my own hands had been anywhere near that small. There was no way anyone in our house could have left tiny handprints like that.

The handprints were the least scary phenomenon, actually, but by far the most prevalent. Something else that occurred on a few occasions was much more disturbing to me (and the rest of my family). In different areas of the house — by my bedroom closet door, in the upper hallway near my sister's room, in the living room, and in the kitchen — small droplets of blood (at least that is what it looked like to everyone who saw it) would suddenly appear and trickle down the wall. It looked so disgusting. There was no reasonable explanation for this; no one in the house had been bleeding, and nothing had been spilled. We all saw it, though, and were all baffled (and somewhat horrified) by it. Usually it could be cleaned up right away. But in the living room it reappeared a few times before we could get rid of it completely.

My sister is a few years older, and a few inches taller, than me and her hair is blonder, so I assumed it was her I saw one morning when I saw a blond girl her size sitting on the floor in the living room staring into the fireplace (it wasn't on at the time). She was angled away from me, so I couldn't see the front of her completely, but it looked like she was eating something out of a bowl in her lap, from my viewpoint.

I wondered why my sister would be eating her breakfast cereal sitting on the floor like that ... and then almost ran right into her as I walked into the kitchen. She was coming in from the other door leading from the family room, which was at the opposite end of the house from the living room. It obviously couldn't have been her I had seen. By the time I got back to the living room there was no trace of the girl by the fireplace.

The ghostly encounter I had in our bathroom is the most remarkable for me still. I was backing up, and not watching where I was going, when I accidentally bumped into the edge of the large Jacuzzi bathtub. That made me lose my balance, and I felt myself start to fall backwards right into the tub. I was so scared. I was positioned so that my head would be hitting directly onto the brass faucets on the other side of the tub, and that probably would have really injured me. I felt so helpless, feeling myself falling like that and knowing there was nothing I could grab on to or any way I could regain my balance. I even remember gritting my teeth and scrunching my eyes closed, waiting for the impact I knew was coming any second.

But then something happened that will forever change the way I feel about spirits. As I hit the back of my knees on the side of the tub and was falling over backwards into it, I felt a very firm and strong arm and hand grab onto my back as I was in mid-air and gently lift me back onto my feet again. I can't even precisely express how amazing that experience was. And I felt enormous gratitude instead of fear.

2

The Haunted Experiences of Others in the United States

Western United States

CHANGE IN THE ATMOSPHERE

We moved into this house that my father bought as an investment property after the previous owner died and left his home and possessions to a boys' facility in the state. It was quite rundown, and my father did a lot of renovations before he asked if my small family would like to move in.

My dad and mom died a year apart, and we inherited the home from their estate. After my youngest daughter was born the next year, things changed in the atmosphere of my home. I was sort of saddened because my parents would not see my youngest grow up, and it all started from there.

Things started appearing in pictures of the baby, but *only* the baby. If anyone else was in a photo with her there would be no anomalies. As she grew the activity increased as well. The things in the pictures went from spots to misty apparitions and green mist. Two pictures had full faces in them.

About the time she turned a year old she started "talking" to the visitors. It seemed that she drew them to her wherever she went. They came to her because she talked to them, played with them, and just basically validated that they were really there.

In restaurants, stores, etc. she would see these people and talk to them as if they were just normal everyday people. One incident happened at an old bed and breakfast we had gone to for lunch. We all sat down, and she told me in a whisper that "EEleena" wanted her shoes and box.

Now we had been used to her doing that sort of thing, so we called the owner over and asked her if there were any ghostly things happening around the restaurant. She brought us the brochure we hadn't noticed before, and it said to ask them about Helena (pronounced *HelEEna*). We promptly told her that our daughter talked to spirits regularly and that Helena wanted her shoes and box.

The lady wondered, "What box?"

The baby responded, "It's a hatbox with pictures and mementoes."

Now she was a fourteen-month-old baby at the time when she said this, and clearly she would not normally go around talking about mementoes or hatboxes. So the lady took her advice. We have not heard if they found her shoes and box yet, though.

When it all started we were skeptical people. We would pass things off and say, "Oh, we didn't see that!" to each other or ourselves, and finally our "visitors" got tired of us not acknowledging that they were there and were real.

On one particular day we had returned home from shopping for groceries and put the kids in their room. We were in the kitchen putting away the food and we heard a noise in the dining room. Thinking the kids had left their room without permission, we walked into the dining room only to find one of their new toys from Christmas running by itself. It was one of those toy racing tracks where you had to squeeze a trigger in order to make the cars go.

The problem was, however, there were no batteries and my husband had disconnected all the wiring to see if he could fix where the cat had chewed part of the wires. The little cars were zooming around with their lights on, but with no obvious form of power.

So we turned around and went back in the kitchen and said, "We didn't see that!" to each other.

A few seconds later we had put an unopened box of spaghetti in the cupboard, and my husband turned his back to the cupboard to reach for something from me. He was hit with a handful of spaghetti from the now open box. The box was empty on the shelf just as it was placed, but the spaghetti flew out. We *then* started to say, "Okay, okay, we believe you are here."

Several other things have happened too. One friend won't visit us anymore as something occurred to her in our home. She was using the bathroom when the shower curtain drew back and the shower head adjusted as if someone was readying for a shower.

***

THE HAUNTED DUPLEX

My husband, child, and I moved into a rundown older house. We moved there because of the cheap rent on the house. It was a converted duplex. Upstairs was our home. There was a basement too, and it was hard to keep renters in there.

Every time you walked in the front door you could smell a strong flowery smell. After we got moved in we would experience slamming doors, the sound of footsteps, our dogs would not come into the house at all, and the gas stove kept being turned on. It was all bearable but nerve-shaking.

The part of the house we had was all right, but in certain spots you would get the feeling like you just should not be there. My daughter slept in our room because her bedroom was always so much colder than the rest of the house.

The landlord asked us to check out the basement because he was going to try to rent it out again, and just walking down the steps you could feel something trying to push you. There was not a good feeling in the basement at all. After we had checked it out and cleaned it up a little bit, he rented again. But the person who rented the house only stayed for two weeks. He told me he could not stand that we walked around all night long and banged on the walls. Of course I tried to tell him that we did not do that at all. After he was gone the activity got worse, so we moved out too.

––––––

PROTECTIVE SPIRITS?

I was born in a haunted house. My mother was abusive, and the spirits would protect me by throwing things in her way when she would try to chase after me. I didn't know it then, but they were helping me. It was a common occurrence to see things fall off the shelves or the radio and lights to go off and on.

Most of the sightings occurred in the basement, where my bedroom was located. We had a rec room down there, and then off of that was my sister's and my bedroom. We would run through the rec room and shut our bedroom door. They would call my name at night and stroke my hair. It would scare the hell out of me because I was a teenager, and my sister had moved out.

Our dogs refused to go down into the basement, but when I would carry them into my room they would follow someone with their eyes, then look at me and whine. I would let them go back upstairs. My mother never came down there. I think she felt that she would be attacked. All kinds of these things would happen all the time.

When my father died and my mother moved to an apartment, I rented the house out. The renter told me one day that her three-year-old said that a man would come and visit him at night and play with him with a toy horse. So she asked me if I ever felt anything unusual about the house. I told her the truth. She was surprised but continued to live there, and the little boy loved the man with the toy horse.

I decided to sell the house. Some friends of mine would not believe that it was haunted. So, before we sold it, I proved to them that the spirits were there by having a seance. We all sat in the basement.

"Hello. These people don't believe that you are here. Can you do something to prove to them that you live here?" I said.

No sooner had I said that than things started crashing to the floor upstairs and downstairs in the storage room. I just sat there and laughed as everyone screamed and ran outside.

"Thank you," I said.

I looked around the house, and sheet board was scattered all over the living room. We had been remodelling it. In the storage room many things were on the floor, so I made my friends clean it up. They wanted proof and they got it.

[After] I sold the house and handed over the keys, I stopped by before the people moved in, but I couldn't get in because it was locked. I stood in the backyard with my head against the door and said goodbye and that I loved them all.

As I drove away, I looked at the house and the lights were blinking on and off. I guess it was their way of saying goodbye.

———

MARY

When I was a boy in the 1960s, I spent summers at my grandparents' farm. My cousins and I probably drove them crazy, but they always seemed happy to have us there.

One night, when I was about ten, I got to stay outside in a tent out back of the house with two of my older cousins. They would have been in their early teens.

My cousin Rick was the oldest of the grandkids, and big for his age. So he helped out more than the rest of us could. And that night he was telling my cousin Ian and I about what he had found in the barn that day when he had been helping to unload the truck.

Granddad had pointed to a spot at the back of the barn for Rick to put the boxes, and as he put them down he knocked over something that had been leaning against the wall. Granddad went over and picked up the heavy stone that had fallen and leaned it against the wall again. He told my cousin that he had found it years ago, when building the house. It was a little girl's tombstone from the 1800s. Part of it was broken, so the last two numbers of the year were missing, but you could still see her age when she died was seven and that her name was Mary.

None of us had ever noticed that old gravestone in there before, because he always kept a large barrel in front of it.

Ian asked Rick if Granddad had told him where she was buried. That question scared me too much, and I decided I didn't want to sleep in the tent, that close to the barn, after all, and ran back into the house without waiting to hear the answer.

The next day the older boys asked Granddad some more about Mary. Thinking about that tombstone out in the barn still scared me, but I felt a bit braver in the daytime, and was kind of curious to hear more too.

Now, you have to understand my grandfather and grandmother were no-nonsense kind of people. They were kind and loving, but always very serious and proper. If they said this happened, then it did. And I've never forgotten what I was told about Mary.

[My grandfather] and my grandmother had bought the land from his parents, when they got married in the 1920s. They built the house as they could afford to, so it took a long time, and they lived with my great-grandparents until it was finished.

One day a neighbour lady (who lived on the other side of the property at that time) came over for a visit. She asked my grandmother who the little girl was in their new house. My grandmother said the house wouldn't be finished for some time yet, and no one should have been in there. The lady told her she had just seen a little girl standing at the front window, on her way past there just then. She could even describe the dress the girl had been wearing, she had seen her so clearly.

When my grandfather got home later that day, my grandmother asked him to go over and check on their house to make sure no one was in it. He found it empty.

Shortly after the birth of their first son, my cousins' dad, the house was finally done. But not long after they moved in, my grandmother woke up one night because she felt someone tugging at the sleeve of her nightgown. She said there was a whitish blue light shining all around and throughout her, and was sure she was the same little girl her neighbour had described seeing. My grandmother was frightened and jumped up in bed, but then she realized she smelled smoke. She momentarily forgot about the little ghost and yelled, "Fire!" to my grandfather, who was still sound asleep beside her.

That got him up pretty quickly, and he told her to get the baby and get outside. A fire had started in the kitchen, and would have destroyed the house, along with the three of them, if they hadn't woken up when they did. But he got to it in time: and no one had been hurt, and their new home was spared except for part of the kitchen.

Afterwards, my grandmother told my grandfather what had woken her up. He then finally showed her the old tombstone that had been found when the foundation of the house was being dug. He had never mentioned it to her before, because he thought it would upset her. But only that stone had ever been found there, no other evidence of a grave.

And it had been his father's farmland since the late 1800s, before he bought it from him. His parents had no idea who Mary was, when they were asked. So, how that tombstone came to be there always remained a mystery, and her ghost was never seen again.

———

Haunted Memories

This actually was the house I grew up in, and I lived there from the time I was one year old until age fifteen.

As far back as I can remember, I was terrified of my room. My mother also had the same creepy feelings associated with this place. My father and brothers mostly wrote off these things as "bad dreams," but Mom always was very understanding and rarely got angry with me when I would start screaming in the middle of the night, or refuse to go to my room after I had fallen asleep in the den.

One half of the room always was cold, even in summer. I would feel things run across me at night, waking me up. This happened probably a dozen times. It felt like a cat or some such animal with sharp nails, but we didn't have a cat when this happened. (Oddly enough, it seemed to stop when we got a cat when I was eleven, so perhaps we had a rat problem? Who knows.)

There also were on occasion small blue — almost pinpoint — lights on my wall near the ceiling. These lights would move around slowly in about a fifteen-inch round area, disappear, and reappear. The intensity was always the same. There was no logical light source for this phenomenon (i.e. it wasn't moonlight dancing on the wall).

When I was fourteen, a boyfriend (who I later found out was very troubled) climbed through my window one summer night to watch me sleep(!). I woke up, having the feeling somebody was staring at me. I freaked and told him to get the hell out or I'd call the police. I found this doubly disturbing because, ever since I was very small, I would wake up to the exact feeling of being stared at, but nothing was there.

When we moved out of this house, I never felt or experienced these things again. I felt very comfortable and at peace in my new bedroom, and every other place I've lived since.

———

PARANORMAL ACTIVITY

Basically, the usual things in a haunting happen: cold spots, voices, the feeling of being watched and touched. Everyone in the house is sensitive to this sort of thing, so it doesn't bother us.

We have a mimic who will sound like the voice of one of us when the person isn't home or hasn't called. Just about daily one of us will hear it. Even friends who don't live in the house have heard it. I will be in my room and my husband will ask if I called him, and I didn't. Everyone in the main room heard my voice from down the hall call him. It happens very often.

I haven't seen an apparition yet, but the children in the house know all of the ghosts' names, who they are, and have seen them. Our children are not given to flights of fancy, so this is not imagination. They have been doing this sort of thing since birth.

Our ghosts are also very opinionated about our friends and will throw things at the people they don't like. Everyone in this house has experienced quite a bit of paranormal activity. This is not the first haunted house we have lived in.

———

House for Sale

I have had lots of experiences in this house. I'll list them from the [oldest] to the most recent.

I saw out of the corner of my eye a small foggy mist floating past just outside our porch, near the ground, when I was walking through the kitchen.

My mother and I were sitting in the living room watching television and suddenly one of two doors in a large hutch opened up slowly. There is a snug clasp inside to keep it shut, yet it was opened effortlessly.

I awoke one morning to see one of my dresser drawers on the floor at the foot of my bed.

My mother walked into the kitchen to see all of our cupboard doors open.

She also walked into the living room once, when she was the only one in the house at the time, and all the cushions of the couch were on the floor.

My mother and I would experience cold touches at night, and hear voices in other rooms of the house.

I was using the restroom one early morning and I heard a man's voice say, "It hurts."

My mom said there were a few nights in a row that she heard what sounded like a pool ball being dropped onto the kitchen floor.

A friend and I once decided to record in this one room where a lot of "touching" happened. Everything was normal, then it sounded like a train was going through the room, and you could hear this deep chanting kind of voice the whole rest of the tape. It was weird.

A few months ago, just before we were to sell the house, my mother said she awoke to find something on top of her holding her down, and she said she got the feeling it was a man.

There was also an incident when our cat was sitting on a chair and looked above the television suddenly and all the hair on his back stood up and his eyes got really big, and then he ran off like someone had scared him suddenly.

The house has a lot of different ghosts. A few are poltergeists, I'm sure, on account of the foolish things like the cupboards and the missing and reappearing items. There are lots of other things that have happened, like a lot of cold spots and touches, and probably more, but there was a point when just my mom lived there. As time went on, the incidents got worse and more frequent.

The house is still for sale, despite being restored.

———

MIDWEST

HAUNTED HOUSEHOLD

I moved back into my dad's house right after he died. He was young when he died, only aged forty-four. I was living alone in the house right after I moved in. When I slept in the living room on the couch, I would wake up all the time, feeling like there was something in the hallway watching me.

My daughter was born six months after this, and I then left the house for a year. I moved back in with my husband, his son, and my daughter almost exactly a year later. As soon as we moved back, things started happening. The first weekend we were there, my cousin said he saw "a small white thing" flying down the hallway.

A year later I had another baby, a son that I named after my late father. My mom was around the first week after I had the baby, and as she was walking into my room to put away some clothes, she saw a receiving blanket falling from the air into my son's empty bassinet, and my cat was watching it intently. She didn't tell me about it at the time because I had company, but she told me about it later.

After that, just little things would happen. For example, objects would suddenly go missing and would be found later in the same spot we had looked a hundred times. About three months after I had my son,

I saw my sister-in-law come out of the bathroom and walk directly into my bedroom and turn on the light. I was curious about that action and asked her if there was anything wrong. She told me that she had seen a man in a white T-shirt standing in my bedroom, but when she flipped on the light nobody was there. I assumed that was my father.

The following year one night my husband said he was running to the store with our neighbour. He left through the front door. About a minute later, I heard the back door open and footsteps go down the basement stairs. I assumed that this was my husband, and he was fetching something out of the basement before he left.

There was silence for about thirty seconds. Then I heard my stepson tearing up the stairs, and I heard him open the back door. Then he came through the kitchen to the hallway, where I was standing, and he wanted to know why I had scared him. I told him I wasn't trying to scare him, I didn't know what he was talking about.

He said that he had been watching television in the basement, and he heard footsteps come down the stairs. He turned his head, expecting to see his father, and instead he said he saw a man with longer hair peeking around the corner at him. He was frozen for a minute, and then the man winked and disappeared around the corner. My stepson ran to the stairs, but there was nobody there. I heard the footsteps, he heard the footsteps, and we both agreed that they were definitely going down the stairs, but neither of us had heard any footsteps coming up the stairs.

We started getting used to the little things that happened, like my kids getting tapped on the head or hearing voices whispering to them. They were all afraid to be alone in the bathroom for some reason.

When I had my last child, I got a baby monitor so I could hear him cry in the bedroom while I had the door shut. Well, I kept the baby monitor on all the time, and when nobody, not even a cat, was in the room, you could hear stuff moving around in there. Even if you couldn't hear anything, I could still see the little line moving on the monitor, obviously picking up sounds I couldn't hear.

A couple of years later, my daughter had lost her tooth. We were putting it up on top of our television cabinet when suddenly the tooth slipped and landed on the floor. I warned my daughter to be more careful, to wait and I would put it up there in the tooth fairy candle case. She didn't listen to me, and just as I thought, the tooth slipped down again, and this time it landed in a pile of blankets and afghans. I was distraught because I thought we would never find the tooth.

I was complaining to my daughter, with my hands in front of me, palms up. I had just finished telling her that we may never find her tooth before the vacuum did when, out of complete thin air, a tooth fell into my open palm. It was her tooth! I was completely astounded! So was my daughter. She was very excited, and kept telling me it was the weirdest thing she had ever seen in her life.

Now, if I had told anyone in my family what had happened, they would not have believed me and would have laughed it off as usual. But luck was on my side that night. My non-believer cousin was at my house (the same person who had the initial ghost sighting in the hallway when I moved back in). He saw the whole thing, and was so distressed that he left. He was very frightened by it. He is a believer now.

Another thing about my house was that sometimes a perfume smell would come out of nowhere. My dad hated perfumes and colognes, so it couldn't have been him. But I like perfumes and aromatherapy, so perhaps it is him, trying to show me love.

Recently my daughter, age six, was going to the basement to tell my stepson something, and as she was going down the stairs she saw a bald man leaning his back on the small couch you could see from the stairs. She didn't continue down the stairs, but came running back up to tell me what she saw. She has told me that she sees ghosts and "other things" all the time, and I believe her.

I am also a ghost hunter, and I often find myself in cemeteries. Well, on one particular cemetery outing, I think I brought something back with me. It was a day trip, so I had my kids along. There seemed to be nothing special about that one; we showed up, cleaned up some graves, and picked up sticks.

The whole time I was there, I was trying to get a rhythm on any energy that may have been around me, but I was unable to pick up anything. I chalked it up to being distracted by the kids. I gathered them up and went home.

The next day, I was sitting on my hallway floor, writing out bills. As I was recording numbers, a strange smell was wafting under my nostrils, strong enough to make me look up from my work. After seeing nothing was amiss, I waved the air and the smell went away.

So, I went back to work, or at least I tried to. I hadn't even made it through another entry when the smell was back, and this time it was enough to make me want to gag. It was so strong I was actually visualizing the smell: it seemed to me like a ribbon that was gliding under my nose. I abandoned my work at that time because someone was at the door, but I wonder what might have happened if I had continued sitting in my hallway.

A few hours later I was able to put my finger on the smell. It smelled like ancient dirt, like a *grave*. I started to suspect that my innocent trip to the cemetery might have had some repercussions.

The next day, I was alone in the bathroom, taking a shower. All of a sudden I had the feeling that I wasn't alone. I tried to shake it off as nerves. Suddenly I saw the shower curtain start moving, and I was aware that I truly wasn't alone.

It was a terrible feeling. Drawing up every bit of courage I could, I told whoever the intruder was to leave me alone, I wanted to take my shower by myself. And then the feeling was gone, the feeling of being watched. But my mind was made up, and as soon as I was done with my shower, I took off to the cemetery I had been to a few days before.

I made several announcements before I left the house, loudly stating that I was heading back to the cemetery, and that anyone who might think they belonged there had to come along. After my cemetery visit, I came home, and my house was like normal again. I have never smelled that smell again or had that watched feeling since.

———

Ghostly Visitors

I grew up in this house. When I was about three years old, I started talking about "the lady on the stairs." She was dressed in an ankle-length black dress with belled sleeves. She was very pale with waist-length black hair. She sat about a third of the way up the stairs, and I was afraid of her. I saw her almost every night.

On one occasion, when I was thirteen, I woke up and someone was lying beside me. I got out of bed very carefully and went toward the door. I looked back, and she was standing on my bed waving her arms. I took off screaming, and my parents turned on the light. That was the last time I saw her.

When I was twelve or so, I woke up one night and saw a man in a brown cloak sitting on my sister's bed. I could see his bare feet and lower legs. He had shoulder-length brown hair and a short beard. He looked like he was about forty years old. He was just watching me, and I was not afraid, just startled a little.

I told my mom about it, and she did a little research on the house. There were once two brothers that lived there. One of the brothers was insane or demented, and would chase people down the road with a knife because he thought the road was his. The other brother took care of him. My mom still hears strange noises in the house, like things falling to the floor and the stairs creaking like someone is going up or down them.

———

Childhood Memories

My mom, my brother, and I moved into the house when I was seven. Before we moved in, my mom and aunt cleaned the house, but when we went the next day and started moving in our things, we found a kitchen drawer full of dirt.

My mom says the first night in the house she woke up in the middle of the night from a sound sleep and said she knew someone was standing in the hall in front of our bedroom doors. She couldn't see anything, but she was paralyzed and covered with cold sweat. She lay there for about five minutes, too scared to get up, and the feeling suddenly went away.

Things happened infrequently over the eleven years we lived there. One night my mom woke up and all the lights in the house were on except the bedroom lights. We got up one morning and every kitchen cupboard door was wide open.

When I was sick I would stay home alone and play in the unfinished basement. I would hear footsteps upstairs in the living/dining room and thought my mom was home. I figured she would be mad that I was playing when I should be resting, so I would run back upstairs, but no one was there. Over and over this would happen ... I would run upstairs and find no one.

When I was a teen I was home one night alone watching television when it suddenly turned to static. I thought the cable went out. Then I realized that I could hear this ugly old art deco clock on the wall ticking ... with no batteries in it. I jumped up, turned off the television, and went to bed.

Another time my friend and I were in my room with the door shut. My mom was at the neighbour's house, and my brother was watching television at the opposite end of the house. We heard a couple of knocks on the door and thought it was my brother bugging us. It happened three more times, and I was getting mad. After the last knock I opened the door to yell at my brother and he answered from the family room. He could not have gotten all the way there in that short period of time.

My neighbour eventually told us that a little boy choked to death in the dining room, right in the spot where the basement smoke alarm would go off when you stepped there. A girl in her early twenties from another family had also killed herself in the garage.

One last occurrence was when my mom remarried and we were going to live at my stepdad's house. My mom and stepdad were doing some last-minute cleaning at around one in the morning before the new people came. The electrical outlet in the dining room suddenly went dead. My stepdad followed the wire up and decided to check in the attic space. He was halfway into the attic when he came down again and said he'd looked into that dark corner of the attic and got a horrible feeling and would not go up there. He is a very sensible and logical man, so something was up there.

In the seventeen years since we lived there, I have kept in touch with our old neighbours. They say that five different families have moved in and out.

Ghost Hunting Experience

After investigating a haunted house in Iowa, I started to experience similar haunting situations in my home as occurred to the girl whose home we investigated. (Coincidentally, the day we investigated her home was also the last day she lived there. She moved out after six months of living there, because the hauntings were unnerving her to the point of needing to see a psychotherapist.)

When I returned home from the investigation, I found myself to be very tired and I lay down for a nap (expecting to sleep thirty to forty-five minutes). I slept very hard and deep, awakening from a sound sleep two hours later. I was hearing a low, eerily whining, whirling wind noise coming from the centre of my bedroom. It was pitch black in my room at the time, so I couldn't see what was causing the noise. But the thought came to me that this was the same type of noise the girl complained of hearing in her bedroom!

I got up, turned on the light, and found no cause for the noise, which had ceased by then as well. I went out into the living room, and was sitting on the couch eating chips and dip when I noticed a small, brilliantly lit golden orb, the size of a dime, appear out of nowhere, approximately three feet out from the TV set and about four feet above the floor. It slowly tracked toward the ceiling light fixture, where it disappeared approximately six inches from the ceiling. That was the first time I had seen an orb with my own eyes!

When I went to bed around 2:00 a.m., I realized that I had not said my opening and closing blessings before conducting the investigation at the other house. I felt that whatever had haunted that girl's home had followed me home, hopefully only to check me out and then leave.

The next morning I got up and took my shower. I towelled off but was still slightly damp. As I walked through a doorway toward my bedroom to get dressed, I felt that I had a ghost clinging to my back. I was enveloped in a large static bubble that caused every damp hair on my back to stand straight up! I turned and walked through the doorway again. The same thing happened again!

When I checked my e-mail messages that day, a colleague, who had accompanied me on the investigation, had sent an e-mail telling of having had a ghost clinging to her back the previous night. It seems that we both encountered the same ghost in our separate homes. I live in northwest Iowa, while my friend lives in southwest Iowa, over one hundred miles away! Do ghosts get frequent flyer miles?

IT'S MY HOUSE NOW

Many times I felt the presence of an older lady in the first house we bought. She lived alone there for many years, and the house was her whole life.

When we bought it, we were redoing the inside, and she was very upset that we were messing up her house. She would slam doors, turn off lights, and turn on water.

One day the dog would not allow me to pass and go into the dining room. Just then, the bookcase flew across the room, like there was an earthquake … and other stuff flew across the room.

I finally said, "This is my house now. You no longer belong here. I love your house, but it is *my* house now."

And from then on she would do little things so I knew she was there, but never "haunted" us anymore. Except one night when we had gone camping a burglar broke in. A neighbour saw this happening, and called the police.

As she was on the phone, the burglar ran out of the house … scared to death … to this day, we think the ghost scared him away!

EXPERIENCES IN OUR HAUNTED HOUSE

We lived in the ninety-year-old house for about six months before we realized it was haunted. The following is a list of some of our experiences:

One night my husband and I were in bed when we saw a shadow move across the hallway. "Are you there?" we both heard someone ask.

When my son was six months old I put him down for a nap. It was ninety-five degrees outside. I went in to check on him, and he was covered in a blanket.

Last summer I woke up freezing. It was so cold in the room, yet we don't have central air and the room air conditioner was not turned on.

When my oldest was two he was in his room and started screaming. He cried, "Lady hair, lady hair," and pointed to the corner.

At about eighteen months my son would point to the corner of the wall and ceiling and say, "What's that?" Then he would start laughing. One time he pointed to the corner and said, "Daddy? Daddy?"

One time we were gone all day. When we came home that evening the faucet in the kitchen sink was on full blast.

My kids' bedroom door always opens and I think one of them is up, but they're not.

My five-year-old says he hears voices in his room.

Once a VCR tape flew off the television.

For two days we kept hearing a *tick-tock*, *tick-tock* sound, and we don't have a clock that tick-tocks.

While I was doing my bills one day I heard a woman scream in the basement; my son heard it too.

I was doing dishes a while ago and I heard a growling sound right behind me; then I heard it again later that week.

———

HAUNTED WORKPLACE AND HOME

Well, first I'll talk about my workplace. I consider it *very* haunted … as do my co-workers! The building where I work used to be a funeral home when it was first built. It is a Victorian-style building, so it looks like an extremely large old house. The room that our office is in used to be the showing room. We can even feel cold spots in there sometimes. There is still the large doorway in the wall that they used to move the coffins in and out, though it has never been opened up in years and years, I'm sure.

We can see reflections of "things" moving around [and] whizzing by us by looking at the reflection of the room on our computer screens. Some have seen objects move by themselves, but I have not personally seen anything move.

I have seen orbs, though — greyish coloured ones — float through the air and then just disappear. You can just sense something in that building. You can also feel that same something in our office.

Recently, I saw two orbs, and a co-worker saw something floating in the air in the back of the office. What she saw, however, was close to the ceiling, and the orbs I saw were midway between the floor and the ceiling.

That same night, I was engulfed by the most frightening feeling I've ever experienced. I was so frightened that I phoned a co-worker and told her of what I saw and how I was feeling at the time. Things like that usually don't bother me at all, but that night, I sure was spooked! I worked in there at night from 10:30 p.m. till 8:30 a.m. alone, so I was pretty much used to the things that went on and the feelings that were there.

I might add that a co-worker of ours was brutally murdered by her husband a few months ago, and right after that is when another of the girls in the office saw the object move by itself. I don't know if that could have been connected or not. We were all quite shaken by her death, and maybe the movement was caused by our own vibes at that time, since we were all so upset and on edge from the entire ordeal. Perhaps it could have been brought on by our emotions. I just don't know.

I have seen shapes out of the corner of my eye. This happens constantly while I'm in the office and there is no one else but me there at the time. I know I am alone because we have to enter a security code to enter and exit the office (the security system makes a buzzer go off and the door can be opened after that), so I would be sure to know if anyone was there!

I feel like there is someone living on the steps that are outside and to the right of our office entrance. The steps are inside the building. They lead down to another floor, which I've never been to. Sometimes when I'm walking by them, I can see a fleeting glimpse of a human shape on them. I can feel a kind of presence around that area.

My family and I can also feel something in our home. When it is dark, I can see things that look like shadows, but yet not quite like shadows. They are somewhat different. It's as if they are blurry. Odd, I know. I can sometimes see someone walk by, but there is no one home but me. There is no distinct figure, but only a kind of shadow. My husband and I see things out of the corner of our eyes around here quite a lot. Nothing we can make out, but it is definite movement of some kind.

We have five cats that live at home with us. They can be standing or lying somewhere and all of a sudden look up (or to the left/right, over my head, to the doorway, etc.) and follow something around with their eyes. A couple of the cats even meow at something sometimes while looking at it.

On Christmas morning, I was taking pictures with my daughter's new camera that she had just unwrapped. It took those really small pictures that you can use as stickers, so I was taking some pictures with it, just to test it out. My husband was watching them develop, and he said, "Look! You have a ghost in this one!"

Sure enough, in one picture there is a kind of light that seems to be right in front of me, on the recliner footrest! I had taken another picture a few seconds after that one was taken and it turned out fine. No strange lights in it at all. Everything was the same. There were no changes in the room, such as lights, no smoke of any kind, no sunshine (as I keep my blinds closed all the time because of the glare that gets on the television and computer screens). Besides, it was early in the morning when that picture was taken and there was no sun up anyway, so we know that didn't cause the film to pick it up! Seeing that picture as it developed gave me a feeling of joy. I had tears in my eyes and called my mother and told her what was on the picture and that I had the impression and feeling that it was my grandpa.

———

A GREAT-GRANDMOTHER VISITING?

My paternal great-grandmother passed away after a long hospitalization. I became pregnant with my first child at the end of that same month, December, but didn't find out until February. My mother has said that it's simply too bad that my grandmother couldn't have known about the baby, because knowing about a new baby in the family would have given her the will to live. In the end, when she died, it was as if my grandmother had just given up.

My daughter was born the following September, and almost right away things started to happen. It was subtle at first ... things you can write off as coincidence or just something weird. First of all, my daughter would not sleep in her crib or bassinet. You could put her in the crib while she was fast asleep, but as soon as you left the room she would be wide awake. What's strange about that is whenever my mother babysat overnight, the baby would peacefully sleep in the crib (identical to our own) that my mother had her at her house.

To keep peace in the household, I started sleeping with the baby on the downstairs living room couch. One night, when she was about two or three weeks old, I was sitting on the couch nursing her. I was very tired, almost nodding off to sleep, when I very distinctly heard someone call my name. There was no one in the house besides myself, the baby, and my husband. I went upstairs to see if my husband wanted something, and he was fast asleep (and didn't appreciate it when I woke him asking, "Did you want something?").

It was around three o'clock in the morning on a cold night, so I don't think someone was playing a trick on me. But I just figured I was overtired and hearing things. As time progressed, I became aware of some very bizarre activity in the house. The thermostat would set itself to ninety degrees. It wouldn't just get extremely warm in the house, the lever on the thermostat would actually have physically moved. My husband and I would go back and forth, thinking the other was turning the heat up. People have now commented on how hot the house always seemed to be, thinking that we were deliberately keeping it that warm for the baby. There was nothing near the thermostat that could have moved it inadvertently, such as a phone cord.

Another strange occurrence was that the inner door off of the front porch would lock itself. We usually did not use the front door because the garage was to the rear of the building, but the front door opened to an enclosed porch, then another door. We did not have a key to this inner door, so we left it unlocked while the outer door was locked when we went out. Many times we would come back, and if for some reason we needed to use the front door, we found that the inner door was locked.

Oddly too, whenever we left the house, the basement light would turn on. This was the incident that really opened my eyes to something being out of the ordinary in the house. It got to the point where both my husband and I would purposefully check the basement light, lock the doors, leave, and joke about how the light was definitely off … only to come home and find the basement light on. Again, there was nothing that could bump the light switch and there wasn't a timer or anything on the light.

My daughter was a very calm, quiet baby. When I would hold her, she would quite solemnly watch things that I could not see. She would move her head and eyes as if watching someone enter the room and walk across it. She would smile as if someone she knew and loved was standing in front of her. One time, I remember she very distinctly seemed to watch an invisible person walk into the room, pace a little bit in front of us, then stop. It was a very uncomfortable feeling because it was not, as my mother explained knowingly, a very young baby learning how to focus her eyes, it was a baby definitely watching someone.

All of the things I have described so far sound strange, but even I can admit that there may possibly be logical explanations behind them. I don't think that's the reason behind what happened, but I do know that I wasn't just imagining the following events. One morning, while I was still sleeping on the couch with the baby, I woke up early to make my husband breakfast before he went to work. Leaving the quilt and pillow I had been using on the couch, I put the baby in her swing and took perhaps two steps into the kitchen. For some reason, I stopped and turned back into the living room. To my great shock, the quilt and blanket were now on an armchair across the room. The heavy quilt was neatly and precisely folded, the pillow placed on top of it. Again, my husband was the only other person in the house, and he was asleep. Even if he had been awake, there was no physical way that someone could have folded the blanket in the two or three seconds my back was turned.

Perhaps a month or two after this, we were having more success at putting our daughter to sleep at night. After placing the sleeping baby in her crib, I was slowly backing out of her room. With no warning, the mobile over her crib started playing as if it had just been wound. It did two complete revolutions, then stopped abruptly.

At that time, I felt very frightened … this was not helped by the powdery perfume smell that suddenly filled the room. I continued backing out of the room and went into our nearby bedroom. But, about a half second later, I dashed back into the baby's room and snatched her up, resigning myself to another night on the couch. We moved from that house the following June.

Since we have moved, I have noticed that while some things have changed, others are still pretty odd. For one, the baby slept through the night in her crib the first night we moved in and has been consistent with sleeping through ever since. Lights stay off when they are supposed to, and doors don't lock themselves. But things go missing around here — keys, hairbrushes, shoes, the remote control — only to be found later in an obvious place. It comes and goes. But that's another story.

———

NORTHEAST

MY CHILDHOOD HOME

This was my childhood home. The house was built for us out in the country in upstate New York, on land that had never been occupied as far as I know. We moved in when I was five. It's a big house on ten acres of land. When I was growing up we had few neighbours, but the area has since been built up.

I don't remember the exact first occurrence, being so small. I often complained to my parents about feeling people in my room. They wrote it off to my being nightmare-prone. One time I woke up when I was about six or seven and saw a dark-haired woman in a white nightgown run across the room, leap onto my bed, and vanish. This was not a dream — I was wide awake.

As I got older, the house spooked both my sister and me. She was five years older than I. The most common occurrence was the sound of footsteps walking around upstairs when no one was up there, always at night. Once I heard whistling (as in a song) coming from my parents' empty bedroom. That bedroom was the centre of most of the activity — the footsteps usually began there and walked down the hallway and later began continuing down the stairway. By standing in our kitchen door, we could watch that stairway as reflected in the front hall windows, and it would be totally empty as the footsteps came down. I was often left alone at night, and I would sometimes become so scared I'd run out on the lawn and wait there till my parents came home.

There was often a feeling of malice, a sense of something invisible and cold in the room. It was also common to hear murmuring voices — more than one — in a distant part of the house when no television or radio was on. As time went on, the occurrences got more blatant — doors began opening by themselves. I don't mean we'd find them open, but that the doorknob would turn and the door would open by itself. Sometimes in the morning it would open my parents' door, walk down the hall, open my door, and walk up to my bed and look at me. I [first] thought it was my father saying goodbye before he went to work (I was in high school by then), but he denied it when I asked him. The next time I opened my eyes and peeked — nothing was there.

Interestingly, the experiences began to intensify as I got ready to leave the house. My senior year of high school was filled with them — sometimes I'd come home from school, grab a Diet Coke, and leave for work, only to find my car keys missing. I'd always find them upstairs in my bedroom, where I hadn't even been. A few times there was a huge boom upstairs — like massive furniture crashing over. Nothing was ever found misplaced.

My nights of waking up to that cold presence in the room became more and more common. A few weeks before I graduated, a friend and I were in my bedroom when my closet door flew off its hinges — we were nowhere near it — and fell right next to where we were standing. The weirdest thing about that, however, was that it landed on the dresser containing all my makeup, hairbrushes, etc. — but when we looked, not only was none of that stuff knocked over, it was all lined up in two perfect rows on the opposite end of the dresser. That really scared us. I graduated from high school and went to college shortly thereafter.

Whenever I came back on Christmas break, I could feel it trying to manifest — I know that sounds crazy, but it was palpable. The footsteps and "presence feelings" continued whenever I was there, but it added some new things, such as electrical appliances turning off and on by themselves.

Again, most of these incidences happened in my parents' bedroom. My mother had a teddy bear collection, and she would complain that a singing one would turn on around 3:00 a.m. and sing a Christmas carol. Another one that was programmed to say a few sentences would also speak out in the dead of the night. Her television often turned on between 2:00 and 4:00 a.m., and when she was watching it during normal hours, it often shut off by itself.

When I was in my late twenties, my older sister became ill and I moved back home to help care for her children. I wasn't as scared this time of the footsteps, presence, etc. The house computer was located in my parents' bedroom, and a few times when I was online, the lights would die, the television would turn off, and so forth. I sort of refused to be scared by it, and that actually seemed to help.

One time when this happened, my computer screen froze and I was getting ready to reboot when on my screen (I was in a word processing program at the time) appeared the sentence: "I am here." That really did scare me to death. But being older, I've realized that whatever this thing does — open doors, walk around, etc. — it doesn't have the power to hurt me, so I try to keep that in mind whenever I visit.

My parents have never experienced any of the phenomena except the stuff in their bedroom, which they write off to "shorts" or strange electromagnetic fields. They don't believe there's anything in the house and think my sister and I are crazy. Recently we were all in the kitchen when there was a ten-second or so birdsong from the (empty, of course) living room — totally bizarre. They just shrugged it off, while my sister and I asked, "You don't think that's strange? You're not curious about the fact that an invisible bird just sang in the living room?"

Most of the experiences seemed to centre around me, and why that is I can't imagine. I was only five when we moved in there. My sister did recently admit that the same footsteps and presence came to her whenever she was alone in the house, but me being younger, I was always home, and so she was rarely alone in the house.

Another odd thing — and this could be coincidence — is that the day after four of my visits home, an animal has been found in the house. Once our cleaning lady found a bat in my bathroom wastebasket, twice enormous snakes slithered through the house from nowhere, and another time a chipmunk was found indoors. They were all alive. We also had a sudden infestation of mice for the first time when I moved back home as an adult, as well as a fire on a night I spent there alone. The cause was never determined.

My niece and nephew have both talked about ghosts appearing to them in the guest room where they spend the night when they sleep over. My nephew, who was about four at the time, was very clear in describing a tall man with long black hair who handed him a feather, then put his fingers to his lips in the "shh" gesture. It sounded like a Native American to me, but my nephew told me he wasn't supposed to talk about it.

My niece, who was five, came into my room at a Christmas visit and complained that the "ghosts" were keeping her awake and she didn't get any sleep. She asked me if they would hurt her. I didn't want to scare her, so I told her to ignore them and say a little prayer when they bothered her. The next day she mentioned them to my sister, who told her they weren't real.

Interestingly, when I was on the phone the next day, my niece kept paraphrasing things that my friend on the telephone was saying, but she was across the room — there was no way she could overhear her. So perhaps she has a bit of psychic talent. I seem to, which perhaps explains why we experience this stuff more.

———

HAUNTING ENCOUNTERS

About a year after my wife and I moved into our home I started to notice orbs appearing in photographs taken around the house, especially those taken of myself. I then purchased a video camera and have recorded numerous anomalies around the house.

My wife and I have also experienced episodes where one of us will wake up in the middle of the night, usually between 3:00 a.m. and 5:00 a.m., to find ourselves paralyzed and unable to move. It only affects us one at a time, and it only happens to one of us if we happen to be sleeping alone. I have awakened on several occasions to the sensation of a force gently pressing down on my chest and legs. I'm usually not afraid of it, and I find that if I try talking to it and ask it to leave me alone it usually dissipates immediately.

Recently, I woke up to feel someone's hands grab both of my wrists. The hands did not hold me down or grab me too tightly, but it definitely had a good hold of me. It felt like two hands with fingers, skin, etc. I told it to knock it off, then got up to go to the bathroom, and it vanished.

My wife had an experience several months ago where she fell asleep in a chair in the living room. She woke up to a loud buzzing sound in her ears and was totally paralyzed. She was unable to move, but was able to look up with her eyes to see a misty white cloud forming above her. It took on the shape of an older man's face. She said it appeared angry with her. She then heard a voice, more in her head than in her ears, saying something along the lines of, "You're ruining things." (As a side note, my wife and I were arguing at the time. I got the impression that the entity was scolding her for it.)

We will also see white blobs or shadows dart out of the corner of our eyes on numerous occasions. Despite the one episode where my wife felt she was being scolded, both of us feel perfectly comfortable living in our home and do not feel that the presences are negative in any way.

A History of Death

We bought a very old apartment building, which had been built as a large home in 1844. It had twenty-eight rooms, which had been divided into six apartments. The remainder of the house was left as one whole side, which we lived in.

Moving in was exciting, as it was old and I loved history, and it was listed in the National Registry. The house had three floors with many stairs and three landings. We had decided to use the large third-floor attic as our son's bedroom. We ordered carpeting to be laid before we moved in.

The two guys who were laying the carpeting were working alone. They had done the job — rather quickly, I noticed — in less than thirty minutes. I asked if they thought the room was nice, as it overlooked the entire historical section of the street.

"Yeah, but this cold breeze you have blowing up these steps and in this room is awful … especially if you're gonna use this for a bedroom," one guy responded.

I asked him what he was talking about. There were no broken windows or doors opened.

"When we were up here it felt like someone left a freezer door open. Girl … I'm glad we're finished," he replied.

I asked why he would say that as the heat was on, and heat rises, and it was quite warm in the house.

"We kept feeling this strong breeze blowing past us, and we're freezing to death!" he told me, and they practically fell down the steps getting out of there.

We moved our son's bedroom furniture up, including the full-flotation waterbed he wanted. We filled the mattress of the waterbed and went downstairs. Our son returned to his room but came running down the stairs, jumping on every other stair to get down.

He said in no way was he sleeping in that room, because of what he just saw — his waterbed being walked on and the "blur" of a small child jumping off the bed and sliding down the wall!

That night he slept in the guest room on the second floor, which we made into his bedroom the next day.

It was a week later that I noticed things starting to happen, and it was always at 10:00 p.m. Our car keys started turning up in bizarre places; the television channels would change with no one holding the remote; the television would switch off and on.

The dog's basket was thrown into the air, and our miniature schnauzer was tortured by something. She would whimper and turn from side to side, as if she was being teased.

If we chose to sleep with a light sheet on us, we would feel bugs crawling all over us, so we slept with heavy blankets. The third floor door would come open on its own, even though it was closed with a latch. We never used the third floor because we *knew* there was something wrong with that top floor.

We would hear something or someone roaming around upstairs, knowing no one was there. Lying in bed we could hear the sound of scraping sounds and things being pushed around. It was as though something really bad had happened there.

My husband is not the ghost-fearing type, but these little bizarre happenings have made a believer out of him ... even more so since the night he was grabbed by the neck, by a warm hand, scaring the bejesus out of him.

In talking to the neighbours, we learned the house had a history of death. A Second World War veteran came home and committed suicide. His mother died on the sidewalk beside the house.

A doctor, who built the house in 1844, had a practice on the top floor. A child died there while in his care.

Since we sold the house, it has been sold three more times. We kept it longer than anyone ever did ... almost five years.

THE BOARDING HOUSE

The boarding house I lived in was over one hundred years old and had a reputation for being haunted. I laughed at the idea of the place being haunted at first. I was an adult (yeah, right, at eighteen I was just a know-it-all teenager!) and nobody could change my mind ... or so I thought.

Things started happening. A door I know I left closed was open in the morning. My radio was turned on after I know I shut it off. And there were all sorts of strange noises in the night. The basement of the house was fixed up with a little kitchen and a billiard room. Well, the first half of the year, there wasn't a pool table in the room, but late at night you could hear billiard balls hitting each other and smell cigar smoke (it was strictly a no-smoking house!). And the dog, this great big, overprotective golden retriever, couldn't be dragged into that room.

It's funny, I can only remember being scared of the house once. In the middle of the day, something tugged on my hair. Now, I had a very short haircut at the time, and I know it wasn't caught on anything.

WHAT'S UNDER THE RUG?

We bought our first house a few months after we got married. My husband likes modern and I like older homes, and we were having trouble finding something we both liked. Finally we found a century house that we both wanted. It needed work (a *lot*), but we thought it was a diamond in the rough and we could handle most of the renovations ourselves. I won't get into the endless trouble that bottomless money pit turned out to be, but I will describe what happened while we were working on it and after we moved in.

We still lived in our apartment as we were fixing up the house, room by room. Most of the time we worked on it together, but sometimes, if I had an extra day off of work, I would be over there alone, taking down old wallpaper or painting.

I began to notice that when I was alone I felt uncomfortable in the master bedroom. No other part of the house bothered me, but that room did. I never liked being in it, especially when I was there alone.

An odd thing was that there was an old section of shag carpet nailed down to a spot on the floor in that bedroom, while all the other floors were bare.

It seemed so odd a previous owner would do something that senseless and damaging to the old floor. They had surrounded it with so many nails it was almost impossible to remove them, and it looked like it had been like that for ages.

Finally, the day came to paint that room and get rid of that carpet. When we arrived to start the work that morning, we found a huge brown stain right in the middle of the rug. It was already very dirty, but that awful stain had not been there before. We were positive of that.

It looked like a large dried pool of blood, and there was a very unpleasant "rusty" smell in the air. We had no idea where that could have suddenly come from. My husband got down on his knees and looked at it more carefully. He confirmed it definitely looked and smelled like dried blood.

I never liked the feeling in that room to begin with; now this discovery was too much for me. I wanted to get the hell out of there and not return. But my husband calmed me down, and we tried to think rationally of what could have caused something like that. Neither of us had been in the room for a couple of days, and we both knew that dried puddle had not been there before.

We were planning to remove the carpet that day anyway, so decided to go ahead with that plan. After a lot of effort we finally got all of the nails pulled out.

As we picked up the carpet we could finally see the floor beneath it. My husband let out a frightened, "Wow," and seeing his reaction scared me as much as what I saw on the floor. The dry stain on the carpet was a brownish colour, but the puddle of liquid, which we assumed was blood, on the floor below looked very fresh and was dark red.

No one had been in the house besides us (and no animals either). There was not a single drop of blood anywhere else, and no broken window or forced entry. Nothing else had been disturbed at all, but I still suggested we should call the police. My husband pointed out that no crime had been committed. We had just found this mess (of blood?) coming up through the floor under a rug that had been nailed down for years, in the middle of an empty room, in the middle of an empty house. What could they do about that, besides delay finishing the house and create a lot of negative attention in our new neighbourhood? I reluctantly agreed that time, but told him I was calling them if we ever saw anything like that again.

I didn't want to live in the house anymore, never mind sleep in that bedroom after that, but the only other bedroom was much too small for us, so we had no choice.

Once it was decorated it looked much better, though, and I slowly started to feel a bit more comfortable. But then one night I woke up and saw a woman in our room, standing in front of the dresser and staring into the large mirror, with her back to me. The streetlights outside lit up that room at night through the window transom, so I saw her plainly. She was only about five feet tall, and had very long, dark hair, and wore a long white nightgown. I could only see her from the back, though, so I couldn't see her face or tell how old she was.

She kept picking up strands of her hair, as though she were admiring them in the mirror. I watched her for at least a minute before she gradually disappeared. I was more astonished than scared, I think.

Both my husband and I have heard footsteps coming into the bedroom, and I've felt someone stroke my hair and pat my arm.

The bedroom was the only place in the house that seemed to be haunted. I did some research and found out that a woman died in our home (in childbirth, so quite probably in our bedroom) in 1912. The baby also died. I was sad to learn that, but that might explain what we experienced there.

SEEING, HEARING, AND FEELING IS BELIEVING

I've seen small apparitions along the floor. We do get mice occasionally, but these were bigger and much faster than a mouse. Not a mole either. Once, and only once, I've seen a dark shadow person almost peeking at me from the living room doorway. I stared at it for a full ten seconds before it disappeared.

I've felt a tap on my left shoulder while at the computer, and often have water drops fall on me from some unknown source.

I've heard voices, calling my name and others' in the family. There are many noises, but only one that I can positively say was not caused by some animal in my attic. I was lying in bed watching television. The attic is right above me. I heard something with weight going across the attic floor stopping directly over my head. Then it went back, quickly. Whatever it was it was very heavy. So heavy, in fact, that I thought at first that my seventeen-year-old son had gone up there just to scare me. He didn't.

I got up and planned on catching him descending from the attic, but he was just in his room playing Nintendo. I sent my husband up there to check for evidence of some large animal. There was none.

I'm not the only one who has experienced things in this house. All of my family, with the exception of my oldest boy, have related their experiences, mostly the same as my own. And that includes my very skeptical husband. But I don't feel in any danger or scared by this.

LADYBUG, LADYBUG ...

My family has experienced many strange things that make us believe our house is indeed haunted. At first we just heard the odd noise, like footsteps or knocking, and that didn't really bother us too much. My kids never seemed to be frightened at all, so I never worried much about it either. But after a while it got even stranger. Many times we would leave the house and come back hours later to find the television was now turned on, loudly, even though everyone was sure it had not been on when we left (we would have heard it if it had been).

One day my young daughter was off school, sick, and was lying on the sofa watching a movie. I was in the kitchen getting her a drink when I heard the sound of the channels on the television being changed. I called in to her and asked why she had changed the movie she was watching, and when she told me she wasn't doing it I glanced into the living room to see what was going on.

The television was in the far corner of the room, and the remote control was on a table in another corner. My daughter was lying on the sofa against the opposite wall, quite a distance away from either the television or the remote control.

It was obvious that she hadn't been the one changing the channels at all. And as I watched the television, this continued to happen. We both looked at the television in wonder as it kept doing it. Finally the movie she had been watching, which was on a tape in the VCR, came back on, and the television acted normal again. It was really amazing how that happened.

My other daughter often heard what sounded to her like someone was singing or chanting, and once saw the figure of someone she said she thought looked like a monk, because he was in a long robe.

But the strangest experience we had was when we decided it might be best to sell the house and move. This wasn't really due so much to the haunting as it was to the location. We wanted to move to another part of the city.

Even though it was December, and very cold and snowy, each time there was an appointment to show the house to prospective buyers our front lawn and porch stairs would become *covered* with ladybugs.

If it had been spring, summer, or fall I don't think this would have been quite as shocking. But to see hundreds of those red little bugs just appearing out of nowhere and crawling through the snow like that was beyond strange. And it was only ever on our property. Never on our next door neighbours' lawns. They confined themselves to our yard, and they only appeared just before people were scheduled for a viewing of the house to see if they wanted to buy it.

Once, when an appointment was arranged for the afternoon, we looked outside expecting to see the ladybugs, but there were none. We assumed it had been a weird coincidence all along, and even though it was so very peculiar that ladybugs would be outside on our lawn in cold winter weather it could not have been related to the sale of the house. But, it turned out, on that particular occasion the people never showed up for the appointment, so maybe that was why the bugs never showed up that time either.

We decided not to move after all, and as soon as the sign was taken down, the ladybugs stopped appearing. Even when the spring arrived we only saw the odd ladybug here and there, as would be normal. Nothing at all like how many appeared in the snow before each appointment to show the house that winter.

I don't know what, if anything, the significance of those ladybugs could have been. But that was one of the most bizarre things I've ever seen in my life, and after all the other strange things that happened there we all felt that was related to the haunting somehow too.

———

SOUTHERN UNITED STATES

PARANORMAL EXPERIENCES

This is the house that I grew up in, so I was probably in my twenties before I actually started considering that my experiences were paranormal in nature.

I would frequently hear noises (that were usual noises), but I'd either be the only one in the house or everyone else was asleep. For instance, the drawers in our kitchen made sort of a grinding, squeaky sound when you opened and closed them. I would hear this noise in the middle of the night (it's a very easily definable noise, but there's nothing else in the house that could have made it), so I'd look outside to see if maybe my brother had come home (he was out late a lot) and he was not home. I never did work up the courage to go out into the hall and look into the kitchen … or to ask the rest of the family if they heard anything.

I would also hear footsteps on the carpet in my room and my parents' room. We had old carpet with sort of a crackly padding underneath, so footsteps were unmistakable.

I also had other experiences after I moved out of the house. I would sometimes go there to do laundry (and have some of Mom's cooking!), and at times when I was alone I would get an overwhelming feeling that I was being watched. I also knew that whatever was watching me *really* wanted me to leave. But other times I wouldn't get that feeling at all. One night, though, I got a terrible feeling that there was something evil in that house that wanted me out immediately. I was so terrified that I left laundry running and left my mom a note saying that I didn't feel well so I'd be back the next night … then I ran out the door to my car. I was afraid to look at the house after I left because I had a feeling that I would see something staring at me.

After I was up the street a bit, I looked back and there was a light on in a room that I had not been in. If the light had been on when I was there, I definitely would have seen it, and I did *not* see it.

My mom has also told me some of her experiences, now that I'm older. She went through a series of freak accidents: she had never been accident prone before and hasn't been since, but she broke her wrist twice in the span of a year. She also fell down (or rather, she felt as though hands pushed her down) in the driveway, and she had to go to the emergency room. A couple of days after that, she was lying in bed and she saw someone walk into my old bedroom. She thought it was my dad, so she called his name several times. When he didn't answer she got worried, so she got up and went into the room. There was no one there. She then heard the back door close — my dad had been outside. After this incident, the freak accidents stopped completely. Needless to say, this really frightened her, so much that she didn't tell anyone for about ten years.

We also had incidents where things would get lost and then reappear in a very noticeable place. There was also an unexplained odour in my bedroom … not very often, but it was an awful odour when it occurred. Reading back over this, my mom's house sounds very spooky! But most of these things were few and far between. Overall, it was a very happy, warm house.

———

YOUNG BELIEVER

Although I'm young, I have seen many strange things in the houses I have lived in. My first home was my grandmother's house. There was a strange woman, probably from around Victorian times, mourning for her son.

There was also a spirit in the main hallway connected to the bathroom. He would follow anyone who exited the bathroom down the hall. When I was younger, I confronted him and followed him instead, and he hasn't followed me since.

In my room upstairs there was a presence who loved to scare me. When I was about seven years old, my grandmother bought me a porcelain doll. I already disliked dolls, and I really didn't like that one because of its eyes. I would turn it around on my shelf so it faced the wall. But every morning it would be facing my bed again. One night I got up after hearing a strange scratching noise, and I saw the doll turn around by itself. Since I was so young, that scared me into crawling into bed with my parents. I did not want to sleep in my own room until they took that doll out. Eventually they put the doll in the basement.

My second house didn't have many ghostly occurrences, just some odd mist that would follow me once in a while. I could tell it was friendly, so I let it be.

My third house had one ghost. It would come from the computer room (which would soon become my new sister's room), walk down the hallway, then stop and look out the window in my room.

After a while it really started to aggravate me, so I kindly told it to leave and shut the door. I said that it would have its room back when I didn't live there anymore. It never entered my room again.

My sister was born a year later. She had to sleep in the room where the ghost entered, but she enjoyed his company. I remember one night looking at him watching my sister fall asleep.

The following year we moved into the house we live in now. My sister, being used to the company at night, won't sleep in her room alone anymore. But now I've had more ghostly visits than ever. I doubt there will be a day I will not see these spirits.

———

OUR HOUSEGUEST

This is an apartment we rent in a complex. From the first day, while the movers were still here, we knew we had a houseguest. Things immediately began getting moved, misplaced, or outright disappearing. Of course, moving day you think this is all normal as everything is just in a big ol' mess.

Well, to this day, a year later, we still have these same problems. Set something down and thirty seconds later it has disappeared. Cabinet doors open on their own, and things inside are rearranged. Nothing really spectacular.

Only once have we ever felt any negative vibrations off our guest, and it was during a fight my partner and I were having over money. For the rest of the night, the house felt very uncomfortable, and we both felt watched. Of course, this was probably only residual energy left from the yelling match earlier. The only truly disconcerting parts of the haunting are the shadows and glimpses of things from the corner of your eye.

My partner and I work opposite shifts, so we each spend a lot of time home alone during the week. We each have seen the moving shadow when there is nothing to either cast a shadow or make it move.

We also see what we call our Casper. This is the person who disappears as we walk into a room. A lot of times we'll walk into a room, especially our home office, and swear someone is in there. Just as quickly we see Casper either move out through a wall or go into a closet with no other exit. Now, these sightings take place in the space of about two seconds. Not even long enough for the eye to start taking in detail, only long enough to see something was there.

_____

GHOSTLY VISITORS

I once saw a woman standing in the doorway to my bedroom. She was only wearing a housedress that snaps up the front. She had shoulder-length hair, but no arms, legs, or face.

My parents bought me a new bedroom suite. Soon tiny handprints started to appear at the top of the mirror. And our schnauzer would watch things that we couldn't see.

My bedroom was moved down into the basement. One morning I woke up in the new room and saw an arm from the elbow down getting ready to knock on my door.

My dad died a few months later on our front porch. Then my grandmother died of a massive heart attack. My sister-in-law saw a mist in our living room that rolled past her twice. She said she knew it was my grandmother. The rest of the family was at the visitation.

I had a ghost hunters society in to investigate. While they were there, the head investigator had his EMF detector going off, and the others were taking pictures. He suddenly yelled and threw his detector down because it had shocked him so badly that it left a burn mark on his hand.

We then went into my old bedroom that had a ceiling fan in it. The ceiling fan started turning clockwise, then it slowed down and started turning counter-clockwise, and then started turning clockwise again. They took pictures of it, but I don't think anything showed up.

About a month later they had an all-night investigation. We had motion detectors set up. The one in the garage went off, so everyone ran out to the garage. Some had cameras and some had camcorders. In the digital camcorders you could see orbs flying everywhere. But you couldn't see them with the naked eye. It was awesome!

I have since bought the house from my mom's estate. The ghosts are still there. They move stuff every once in a while. They even left a bunch of potting soil on my kitchen floor in front of the stove … and I don't own one single plant.

I just wish my ghosts would communicate with me. My kids are scared to go to the bathroom by themselves. I think if we knew what the ghosts wanted maybe we could help them. But until then ...

Our Haunted House

It all began shortly after we moved in to this house (we still live here) and started to hear very heavy footsteps sounding as if someone or something very large was walking on the roof. It would wake my daughter up it was so loud.

Very soon after that, things became more and more pronounced, to the point that we called on a Catholic priest to bless the house. That seemed to help with the negative energy, but only for a short time. Doors would open and close on their own, water turned itself on, cabinets opened and closed, the television turned itself off and on and changed channels.

We tried to do some research on the property and get the history of the land but ran into dead ends. Finally, we contacted a local newspaper reporter in an effort to get some tips on getting the history of the place. He was very intrigued and wrote a front-page article on the house. Soon, the producer of *The View* contacted us, and they flew us to New York and paid for everything to have us on their show and tell about our house. They hired a very well-known psychic to come to the house and appear on the show with us.

The psychic told me who one of the spirits was and speculated about the other. One was definitely my grandmother. The other, he felt, was my dad, but he wasn't sure. He described my grandmother to a T, without seeing any photos or anything. I have my own guesses about why she was here. We did not get close until only a few years before her death. She never liked me when I was growing up. After I got older and had children I would take them to visit her, and she thought the world of them. That's when we became close. I feel like she felt she needed to make up for lost time. The psychic told me she wanted to protect my children.

My son told me lots of times, before the psychic ever came here, that he felt like someone had kissed his forehead after he went to bed.

The psychic said there were a lot of spirits here. He told me that my aura was wide open at the top and was like a funnel. He claims that, basically, that's like having a neon sign turned on to the spirit world saying, "I can help." He said there was a whole line of spirits outside of my house waiting in line to get in. I have found this to be true.

One of our pet cats was killed by one of the spirits that was here. We witnessed the cat being "kicked" down the stairs several times. We also witnessed a bird (in its cage) being picked up off the table and thrown across the room.

We have heard very loud knocking sounds, like someone knocking on a door, only it was like the sound was coming from inside the walls, and it echoed. We have also heard a heartbeat sound that filled the entire room. The kids have felt someone brush their hair back and kiss their foreheads. The dogs have growled at the air, the cats have hissed at nothing.

We are constantly being plagued with spirits coming and going. Right now we have a ghost cat; this is only the second animal spirit I have ever experienced. My husband and I have both heard it jump down from the countertops; our cats are not allowed there, and when we heard it we looked immediately and saw nothing. We have also both seen its shadow, and my children have heard certain cat noises with no explanation.

My Grandmother's Haunted House

The house is my grandmother's, and I have known all my life that it was haunted. My grandmother has had three sons die at a very young age, and they are not quite ready to move on and leave their family behind. I have had so many strange experiences in that house.

For instance, around four o'clock in the morning I often hear heavy footsteps coming from the living room through the dining room and entering the bathroom before they disappear. This does not happen every morning, but I would guess probably two to three times a week. I have never seen the apparition behind the footsteps, but my grandmother and sister believe it is my uncle. He drowned at a local lake in 1982. Before his death he would come over every morning at 4:00 a.m. to pick up my grandfather so they could ride to work together. Upon entering the house he would walk through the living room and pass through the dining room and go into the bathroom without fail.

Another example of the hauntings is that my other uncle (who was in a wheelchair) can still be heard rolling through the house in the middle of the night. There were times that I would be in bed and hear the icebox door open, and then see the light come on. I would get up to check and see if my grandmother needed anything, and she would be in bed sound asleep.

My mother has also heard my uncle late at night. After he passed away in 1994, my parents moved in to help with all the bills. Soon after they moved in, my mother started hearing him late at night. She would get up to check on me, but I would be in bed asleep. The morning after she would always ask me if I got up during the night, and she was always surprised to find out that I never did.

The bedroom that is now my parents' was my uncle's at the time of his death; in fact, he died in that room. My mother has told me that she can feel him breathing on her sometimes as if he was lying next to her in the bed. She can also still smell him. He was very ill for a long time, and due to this, when you went into his bedroom you could smell his distinct body odour. You could smell death, and she can still smell that awful odour from time to time.

The most awesome haunting with regards to that uncle is happening with the neighbour next door. I went over to my grandmother's one afternoon this past summer, and the little girl that lives next door was talking. I thought she might have been talking to me, so I said, "I'm sorry, sweetie, what did you say?"

She said she was not talking to me. So I asked her who she was talking to, and the following is my account of what happened that amazing afternoon.

"Who are you talking to, then?" I said.

"You can't see that man?" she said.

"No," I said.

"He is sitting right there in a wheelchair, but everybody says they can't see him. I am the only one that can see him. He told me that he used to live in your house, and he misses it very much. He says that he just wants to find out how everyone is doing, but no one else can see him. So he comes to me so I can find out for him. He has told me what his real name is, but everyone has always called him another name," she said.

When the little neighbour then told me the correct names for him I just gasped. I could not believe that she was actually talking to my uncle, who has been dead since 1994. The real kicker about this is that the little girl is only five years old. She was born in 1996. She never even knew him.

———

MY GREAT-GRANDMOTHER

Generally speaking, I avoid houses that seem haunted like the plague. However, I was not able to avoid the spirit of my great-grandmother as she stayed on as a friendly presence, mainly in the homes of her daughters, where as a young child I spent a great deal of time.

Until the age of six, I spent my days with my great-aunt, who made weekly trips to the graveyard to tend to the plot where her parents lie. We would return to her home, and I would play by myself for hours at a time, except that I was aware of a benign presence watching over me. Occasionally we would play hide-and-seek.

There was a closet in which my great-uncle kept his rifles, and every time I would go in there, it would be icy cold — and in that area of Florida, it is rarely icy cold anywhere at any time of the year. I developed a fear of the closet, but now I know it was just my great-grandmother protecting me from my own curiosity.

My great-grandmother is not bound to any one place on the earth and seems to come and go when needed. One of the most impressive appearances she made was when I was unaware that I was pregnant with my oldest child. I was sitting there alone, smoking cigarettes and drinking wine, when she just materialized … a wispy, shadowy presence, but very strong. She spoke to me through telepathy and told me I was "carrying life." I was not due to have my period for a full week, so I had to wait several days before taking a pregnancy test … and sure enough, I was pregnant.

Interestingly enough, the baby was born on my great-grandfather's birthday, which is also the anniversary of my great-grandmother's death. And even more interesting, my niece was born three months later, on the anniversary of my great-grandfather's death. I found this to be such a curious synchronicity that I have a photograph of myself and my daughter sitting on the tombstone, where the dates are clearly seen.

Other than that, I have had many experiences with non-family ghosts and hauntings, but in general, I stay away from houses that give me that feeling. The house I live in now was briefly haunted by the father of the woman who sold the house to us, because apparently he felt like the guardian or caretaker of the property. He didn't stay very long, though. I addressed him lovingly and told him his watch was over and that he could go on. I would not be at all surprised to find him wherever his daughter may be, watching over her and her interests.

HOME SWEET HOME

I lived in a haunted house as I was growing up. My parents never liked us to tell anyone about it back then. In a house with six kids it wasn't easy keeping this quiet. I'm sure we all told our best friends about it over the years. I know I did. And some of them were there when scary things happened, so they knew it was haunted, and either thought it was great or were afraid to be in the house after that. But we did try to keep it to ourselves and just learned to live with it.

When my oldest brother was about fifteen he was off school, sick, and home by himself. The rest of us were at school, and my parents were working. He was lying on the couch in the family room, watching TV, and had fallen asleep. He felt someone sit down on the couch beside him and place their hand on his forehead. He didn't even open his eyes at first because he assumed it was our mom home to check in on him, like she would always do when we were sick. But finally, when she didn't say anything, he opened his eyes and realized that even though he still felt the cold hand on his forehead no one was there. No one he could see, anyway. He let out a scream, and the hand was immediately gone.

Our dog came running into the family room to see him when she heard him yell, and as soon as she got close to where he was lying on the couch she started to make a high-pitched whine like he had never heard before and kept staring at a space directly over where he was lying. He said she scared him more than the ghost did.

When my oldest sister was old enough to babysit us, so I guess about thirteen, my younger brother and I were home with her one night. We were watching TV and playing cards.

The TV kept turning itself on and off. At first we thought it was just a power problem or because it was a pretty old TV set, so I just turned it back on again and we didn't give it too much thought. But a few minutes later it did it again. I looked over at my sister with raised eyebrows but didn't say a thing, because we tried not to make a big deal about the house being haunted in front of our little brother. He got scared too easily.

She walked across the room and turned the TV on again, and stood by it for a minute or two making sure it would stay on before she sat down again. It did, so she sat back down. When it happened the third time our little brother started to become more aware of what was going on. We told him not to worry, that we would fix it. But neither of us had any idea how to fix something like that.

My sister went over to the television again and knelt down in front of it as she turned it on. The minute she did that our stereo, on the other side of the room, turned on. We all jumped up and ran out of the room, yelling our heads off.

Another sister was home from school with some friends one time and they were just sitting around listening to music and talking. One of the girls left the room to use the bathroom down the hall. She came back and asked my sister why the water was running in the tub. No one but my sister and her friends had been home yet that afternoon, so no one could have turned on the tap beforehand. The girls there that day all swore none of them had gone anywhere near the bathroom until the first girl told my sister the tap was running. And the funny thing was the plug was in the tub and it was about half full by the time my sister turned it off. But if it had been left on all day, since anyone else had been in the house that morning, it would have overflowed and flooded the whole lower level of our house. It must have just been turned on shortly before it was seen, but no one in the house had been into the bathroom to do that.

One time my youngest sister was in the hallway fixing her hair in the large mirror there when she saw someone walk up behind her, but she couldn't see who it was and just saw their arm behind her in the mirror. She finished putting in her barrettes and then stepped aside, thinking it was one of us needing to use the mirror to get ready for school too. But it wasn't one of us; it was a small old man standing there, staring at her. She saw him up close, because when she moved sideways and out of his way she then saw his full reflection in the mirror. But by the time she took her eyes off of his reflection and turned her head to see him beside her, he was gone.

My parents sold that house a long time ago. I wonder if any of the new owners have had any trouble living there? We still sometimes talk about those days when we all get together again. We can laugh now at some of the reactions we had, and how scared we got, but some of those memories still make us shiver.

Ancestor Worship

My husband practises ancestor worship. Basically, he honours his ancestors and in turn they protect us and watch over us. The last count we had of the "people" around us was by a complete stranger (an ancient Chinese man) who asked my husband why he had forty people following him around. Amazingly, that is the exact number of spirits that *should* be following us around. The stranger had never met my husband or knew anything about us.

So our ghosts are not evil or disruptive; they are family watching over us. I have only seen one of his ancestors in full form: his grandmother sitting in the corner just after we got married.

The most fantastic experience was when my child was eight months old and was *walking* down the hall holding onto invisible fingers for support. He did not start really walking on his own for another three months! From the age of two to three, he used to talk to the "white people" on the ceiling, although now that he is older he does not remember doing this.

Now I hear walking all the time. Doors opening and shutting. Most recently the thermostat changed temperature by about ten degrees when I was the only one in the house! Other than that they usually just take my stuff, so of course things go missing all the time, or they play with the kids.

———

DREAMS

I have never seen a spirit while awake, and quite honestly the thought of that scares me. But they seem to come to me in my dreams all the time. Maybe it would be too unsettling to see one otherwise, and this is the best way for them to communicate with me. I've never been frightened in the dreams. Even when I see someone I know has passed away I am so happy to see them again, not frightened at all; [I don't] even think of them as a ghost.

But whenever I do see my loved ones again in this way, it usually foretells some very important event. Sometimes I am told things I couldn't possibly know, so it can't just be my own subconscious mind projecting ideas into my dreams. And sometimes there isn't any talking at all. Just a smile or embrace, and I awake feeling comforted and peaceful. And even though I can rarely remember my dreams, these ones have such a different quality to them that I recall and retain every detail.

The first time I remember having a dream like this was in my early teens. My baby nephew was very sick and had to have heart surgery. We were all very worried about him and so afraid he wouldn't survive the operation.

A few days before his operation was scheduled I had a dream that my dad and my late uncle were fishing. I was on the dock at our cottage watching them and feeling so happy to see them together again, because my uncle had died a few years earlier and my dad missed him very much.

When they returned to the dock and got out of the boat my dad proudly showed me the fish he caught and my uncle gave me a warm hug. I told him it was so good to see him again. He hugged me again and whispered into my ear, "Don't worry, sweetheart, I'll take good care of him."

I told my mom about that dream, and she hoped it wasn't a premonition about my little nephew, thinking my uncle was referring to taking care of the baby if/when he died. My nephew recovered well from his operation, to all of our immense relief. But my father died suddenly of heart failure shortly after that. It comforts me to know he's with his brother now.

This is the best dream I've ever had. In the dream, I was getting an X-ray, and before the technician took it she asked if it was possible that I could be pregnant. I told her no, it wasn't possible (we had been trying for years without luck).

My grandmother (who died when I was little) knocked on the door of the room. I was amazed when I realized who it was, but elated to see her again. She asked the technician if she could talk to me for a minute, and the woman nodded her head and left the room.

My grandmother came over to me and said, "Yes, you are pregnant" and squeezed my hand. She gave me a quick peck on the cheek and giggled. I couldn't remember her ever giggling like that before (she kind of scared me as a kid because she was so stern), and that made me start to giggle too. Soon we were both roaring with laughter. It was such a great moment, laughing like that with my grandmother and both being so overjoyed about the baby.

I was still smiling when I woke up and couldn't wait to tell my mom about that dream. (I think she started crocheting baby clothes that very minute.) And she was right. I was very early into my pregnancy; in fact, it was still so early the first test had to be taken again, but the second one confirmed it was true. We named our daughter after my grandmother.

There have been many others, but the last dream I will mention happened when I was away at university. I had two term papers due on the same day and had pulled an all-nighter getting them finished. When I handed them in I went home, exhausted, and fell asleep. I had a dream that my best friend from when I was in kindergarten was playing hopscotch with me (our favourite game when we were little).

In the dream we were little kids again, and all that mattered in our lives at that moment was playing that game and having fun together … there were no pressures like I was feeling in my current life just then. I woke up feeling much better, and couldn't stop thinking about that dream. I thought it was my mind's way of escaping back to a simpler time, because I was feeling so stressed.

I hadn't seen my friend for years. Her family moved away and we lost touch, but I had never forgotten her, and I planned to track down a phone number for her so we could talk again (before the days of the Internet when that would have been so simple).

But my mom called me later that week. She started the conversation with, "Do you remember Holly?"

I said, "I just dreamt about her a couple of days ago!" thinking that was such a coincidence when we hadn't seen her in over ten years. But the silence at the end of the line told me bad news was coming. My friend had been killed in a car accident on the same morning of my dream.

3

THE HAUNTED EXPERIENCES OF OTHERS IN THE UNITED KINGDOM

THE RED-HAIRED BOY

The house in question was my childhood home, and a happy one at that. We are a family of six with all of the usual ups and downs. I think that things started to happen to me first, but my mum, I think, knew all along. Her family is one of those who have always received warnings about deaths — you know, the usual, pictures jumping off walls, etc.

Anyway, I am the eldest and was going through adolescence at the time. Frequently, I would feel a *whoosh* going past me and the strong scent of roses. It was peaceful. Other things, however, were not.

At first it was fascinating. One of my dad's trophies for football would move around by itself, even when it was placed behind other objects. There were noises of people going up the stairs. My mum's continual denial, I suppose, put me at ease, but when my sister was pushed off a bench in the kitchen my hackles went up.

She was only five, and it upset her greatly. Soon after these occurrences started, we moved out, but it was not due to the goings-on — simply a house upgrade.

I had convinced myself that I was nuts until, as we got in the car, I caught my mum saying goodbye to a person in the house. She denied it, of course, until recently.

It turns out that the previous owners had a son, who was a child genius. Horrifically, he killed himself in one of the bedrooms of our house. This was my brother's bedroom. The reason why my mum denied everything was so as not to scare us. However, she said that was becoming increasingly difficult when my brother kept asking her who the red-haired boy in the corner of his room at night was.

I like to think that since most of the occurrences happened around about the time that we were due to move that the little boy's spirit was reluctant to see us go.

———

SENSITIVE

I am a very sensitive person anyway, but I visited my friend's house, and the night I arrived we were sitting in the lounge.

I had my soul cards out (a bit like tarot), and the lights started flashing; my friend had spent I think around £2,000 to get the electric fixed, so it wasn't that. The air became very cold and icy. I had an unusual sensation in my head, and I felt rather light-headed. I asked my friend to feel around my crown area, and she went to, but her dog placed its paw on her hand, as if preventing her from doing so.

I went to bed and felt like it was winter outside, I was breathing in such cold air. The next day I went to brush my teeth and the lights started flashing.

After a couple of days a friend of ours came over, and we sat in the kitchen. He is very skeptical. As we sat I became aware of an amazing headache, and I felt so hot I went bright red in the face. My friend, a seven-foot-tall man, turned and said that was how he was feeling. The next thing I knew he was in tears, wailing, and said he saw a spirit and it had been such a shock to him.

He described one of the ghosts haunting the house down to what he was wearing. He was really crying, so I gave him some healing. He finally calmed down, and we went into the sitting room. All the pictures there were tilted around a forty-five-degree angle. The light was tilted too.

That next night my friend and I did a cleansing and asked the lost souls to leave. I heard someone wail, and my friend who can hear spirits said the older man was unsure and didn't want to leave. I think they are still there. My friend doesn't, though, as she hasn't had any activity; yet she hadn't had any prior to my visit, either. It is a very haunted house.

THE OLD STONE COTTAGE

My husband and I once lived in a very old stone cottage in the same village in which we still live. A nice old couple now occupies that same home. I've met up with them several times since we moved out and they moved in, and as far as I know they are happy there. But I will tell you what happened when we lived there for over a year, about six years ago.

We had just been married. And it was only the two of us who lived there, with our dog, a German shepherd named Jericho. He was a gift from my husband, because he worked many nights away from home and thought I'd enjoy the company. Jericho was massive, and no intruder would ever get into that house with him on guard ... or so we thought.

We were happy in our first home, except for one problem. It was haunted. One night it was so scary I called my husband at work, begging him to come home right away. He knew from my voice that I was quite serious and something must have upset me terribly to make such a request. When he got home every light in the house was lit, and Jericho and I were barricaded in the bedroom.

When my husband had left for work that evening I had taken Jericho for a walk through the village to visit our friends, but they were not at home. So when I returned back home, sooner than expected and just a few minutes after my husband's departure, I thought he had come back again for something he had forgotten, and wasn't frightened at first when I saw someone's shadow pass by the window curtain as I walked up the laneway toward the door. I could hear loud noises in the kitchen when I walked in and wondered what my husband was doing to cause all that commotion. When I called out to him the noises suddenly stopped, and of course it hadn't been him at all.

When I walked into the kitchen everything was in its place, although it had sounded like every drawer and cupboard was being pulled opened, slammed shut, and rummaged through. I looked about, trying to make sense of it all, and there was Jericho, who usually never left my side, backed into the far corner of the room, cowering and whimpering pathetically.

The dog's reaction only struck me as almost comical afterwards (so much for my big, brave protector).

After being sure that no one else was in the cottage, I bolted the door and sat down in the lounge to do some reading for a while. The dog remained in the corner, refusing to come to me even when I called to him, so I ignored him and read my book.

After a while a movement caught my eye, and I looked up to see what looked like a dense patch of fog, roughly in the shape of a person, floating right toward me. Jericho watched it but never made a sound. As this misty figure floated in front of me, the radio beside my chair started to make crackling sounds even though it was turned off.

[The mist] slowly diminished in size until it was gone. Time seemed to stand still, but realistically I'd estimate it was probably only there for a few very long seconds. But it wasn't so fleeting that I didn't have enough time to study it and to be sure it wasn't just my imagination. It was definitely some kind of entity. We stayed in the bedroom until my husband returned home that night.

At first I was frightened to stay alone in the cottage at night. And that was so unlike me. I have never been a timid person, but I was frightened by that thing. Nothing else happened for the longest time, and eventually I stopped feeling so nervous, even though I often felt like I was being watched.

My husband has always liked to tease me, and he certainly did some teasing at my expense during that time. He had never heard or seen anything unusual himself and never believed in that sort of thing to begin with. But he would always sneak up behind me and say, "Boo" in my ear, trying to get a rise out of me.

One day I came home a bit later than expected and found him pacing nervously in the lounge. I asked him why he was acting so jumpy, and he told me what had happened to him when he had returned home. He heard who he thought was me moving things around in our bedroom. And, as he thought it was funny to do, he quietly opened up the door, preparing to jump in the room and scare me out of my wits. But the joke was on him that time, because it wasn't me he had been hearing. I wasn't even home.

He turned the doorknob, swung it open, and yelled out his usual, "Boo." He saw a blur of motion on the other side of the room, and then all was quiet and he stood there alone.

Nothing was disturbed in the bedroom, but he said he had been sure I was in there moving the furniture around because it had been so loud.

By the time I did get home he was still slightly shaken. After he told me what had happened to him he said he was sorry he had ever doubted me.

———

Our Haunted Home

We moved in here after buying it from an old couple. The first thing I heard was water splashing about around five o'clock in the morning. After questioning my family I found out no one had been awake at that time. Shortly after that, I was washing cement off the floor in a room that was treated for dampness, and distinctly felt something touch my leg. Since then, I have been poked in the back and had someone stroke my hair when I was lying down.

I have seen a figure in the hallway and thought it was my son, who is disabled and tends to stand in my way a bit. So I walked around him. But my son was in the kitchen.

Another time, I was waiting for my younger daughter to return from London. My eldest daughter and I were sitting in the lounge, and we both heard a child's voice call "Ma!" twice. I jumped up thinking she had returned, but there was no one there.

On another occasion, I was eating my tea in the kitchen with my son. We both heard a man's voice shout, "Hello!" twice. Our two dogs ran out into the hall and returned.

My husband came out and asked, "Why did you not go and see who it was?" But I knew it was not a person, as the dogs came back.

Another time I went out around lunchtime, came home, and was asked why I had put silk flower blooms in the toilet. Which, I can assure you, I did not do.

My mother-in-law will not sleep alone here either, as she saw an old lady in a nightie with a bonnet on her head, and thought it was me.

The old lady I bought the house from asked me recently if they called out to me. She had the same experiences. Things are quiet now, unless I get visitors, who then are too scared to return. One young man picked up on my unseen residents straight away and even told me about a suicide, which I knew about, that happened at the back of my cottage twenty-odd years ago. I had told no one of that.

4

PARANORMAL PROFESSIONALS

Something so intriguing about the paranormal is the universal appeal it has for people from all places, all ages, and all walks of life. The professionals interviewed for this book are from across North America and the United Kingdom, and were chosen for their diversity and their mutual dedication. They explain why they have taken such a personal interest in this topic and how they have pursued that interest.

Whether scary, humorous, or very moving, they have great stories and insight to impart, which illustrate why they are so committed to this fascinating subject. Sharing not only the knowledge and wisdom they have acquired but also personal paranormal encounters they have had, their words are entertaining and engrossing, but mostly enlightening.

———

INTRODUCTIONS AND PARANORMAL EXPERIENCES

HEATHER ANDERSON — PARANORMAL INVESTIGATOR, PARANORMAL STUDIES AND INVESTIGATIONS CANADA

I was born in Vancouver, British Columbia, and was adopted into a wonderful family as an infant. Since becoming an adult, I have reunited with both birth parents, and I think it explains a lot about my interest in the paranormal — especially in ghosts and hauntings, past lives and historical studies. My biological grandfather had similar interests and, newly discovered to me, had been heavily involved with the past life regression of a young girl from Orillia, Ontario. These events were eventually written about by author Jess Stearn in his book *The Search for the Girl with the Blue Eyes.*

In high school, I had a wonderful social studies teacher who brought alive the history of Moodyville, North Vancouver, to his students. Since that time, I have involved myself in researching the histories of early Vancouver, North Vancouver, Maple Ridge, the Fraser Valley, and also Bermuda, where I lived with my young family for several years.

I moved back to Canada in 2000 and settled in Maple Ridge with my family. Although I had had some odd experiences as a teenager in North Vancouver, at one time I felt I had to "grow up" and let go of my beliefs in ghosts and hauntings. However, I noticed that many people were still talking openly about ghostly experiences that they'd had. Intrigued by this, and realizing that there was no disputing these personal experiences, I searched the Internet and found a Canadian group I could contribute to, collecting stories and interviewing people all over British Columbia. In 2000, I became Director of British Columbia Ghosts and Hauntings Research Society. In 2005, BCGHRS joined other national research groups to form Paranormal Studies and Investigations Canada (PSICAN), a Canadian-based educational organization where I am now an executive director for the western Canada region.

I have been a regular guest presenter at Langara College, and I have also been interviewed at BCIT radio as well as the Beat 93.5. I was also a guest on CKNW's *The Christy Clark Show*, TV's *Global News*, and I have been interviewed numerous times by the *Vancouver Sun*, the *Province*, and the *Maple Ridge Times*.

———

As a researcher/investigator, I have met numerous people through this interest. Early in our ventures, we met with a witness who claimed the entire apartment building she lived in was haunted, but that her own unit was specifically haunted by children. Through numerous interviews and visits with her, we discovered that she had recently lost two young children to illness, as well as her beloved husband, all within a year of one another. This had a profound effect on me, as it was clear to me that she felt a deep desire to believe her children and husband were still with her in spirit. I came to the realization that ghosts and hauntings, although fun to talk about around a campfire, have sometimes a lasting effect on those who have lost loved ones, and we must continue to respect the dead as well as the living.

———

RONA ANDERSON — PARANORMAL INVESTIGATOR AND PSYCHIC MEDIUM, THE PARANORMAL EXPLORERS

I communicate with earthbound spirits and am a spirit-removal specialist. I'm also a mixed-media artist, cemetery photographer, amateur stand-up comedian, and professional belly dancer.

I started communicating with spirits when I was a toddler and grew up seeing and hearing paranormal phenomena from spirits to UFOs.

I met my husband, Ben Myckan, who is the other part of The Paranormal Explorers, in 1982. With our interest in the paranormal, we originally got involved with a group of people and started doing investigations from 2003 to 2005. We gradually separated from the group and began a serious involvement with investigations, speaking engagements, radio shows, TV interviews, and spirit removals. We did research for the TV show *Creepy Canada*, and I have written an article for *Bite Me* magazine on our investigation in the Edinburgh Vaults. I've also contributed pages of our investigations in Edmonton to the *Encyclopedia of Haunted Places: Ghostly Locales from Around the World* by Jeff Belanger.

We've travelled to England, Scotland, Paris, New Orleans, Nevada, Ontario, and Western Canada to do investigations. Our equipment can fill the back of a spacious SUV. We also own hearses. Go figure.

———————

The most memorable and emotional experience I have had was when I was called to go to this woman's house for a second time to do a spirit removal. Her boyfriend was petrified about going into the basement to do laundry because he was being touched in inappropriate places. The woman had been choked in her sleep, and her son was seeing shadows and having covers pulled off at night.

I went to their two-storey townhouse with a medium I'll call C, who was afraid of ghosts. We discovered a negative spirit in the basement who was possibly a rapist and abuser who was attracted by the woman's "victim energy." She had been terribly abused as a child and young adult and hadn't had proper counselling yet, so her energy was very palpable and was attracting negative spirits.

In the son's bedroom on the second floor, there were three child spirits. Jacob was six, Melissa was ten, and Annabelle was seventeen. Jacob had accidentally set their house on fire (I'm assuming parents weren't home at the time), and he had burned to death and his sisters died of smoke inhalation. The spirits were protecting the boy and hadn't crossed over because Jacob was afraid his parents were mad at him.

So we went to the basement to send the male spirit into the light. I found out his mother was the most important person in his life, so I asked for her to come out of the light and help him in. When she came out, she walked over and grabbed his hand, and he immediately became a thirteen-year-old boy. Then she walked him into the light.

Then we went back up the stairs to the boy's room and told the children the bad man was gone and they didn't have to protect the boy anymore. I was going to bring out their parents from the light because they have been waiting for them (my spirit guide told me that). So the light opened up (I always see it as a tunnel with a ramp going up to a door with bright white light), and the parents ran down the ramp and grabbed the kids and hugged and kissed them. The love was so overwhelming and indescribable.

I never talked out loud about what was happening, and C became emotional and started telling me what she was seeing, which was exactly what I was seeing. She said, "I can't believe you do this. It's beautiful."

I told the woman who was our client what had happened, and she became extremely emotional and then all three of us were crying.

She told me later when her son came home from school he remarked, "Hey, the kids are gone," and her boyfriend noticed the basement felt totally different and he wasn't afraid anymore. The woman's son was unhappy the kids weren't there anymore, and she comforted him by telling him their parents had come to get them and then he was understanding.

It was an amazing spiritual experience.

—————

STEPHEN BOSTON — PARANORMAL INVESTIGATOR AND TECHNICAL TRAINER, SOUTHERN PARANORMAL UK

I am thirty-two years of age from Southampton in the United Kingdom. I work with Southern Paranormal UK on the tech team and as technical trainer, helping new members learn about the equipment we use. I have been interested in the paranormal for as long as I can remember, since a child really. For a short time in the late 1990s I was part of a small team that photographed and investigated crop circle phenomena in Wiltshire. After this, my interests in all fields of the paranormal remained very active; however, hauntings and ghosts had always been my main passion.

Just over two years ago I began looking about on the Internet and researching how to join a real investigation team. I found SPUK and applied. I was interested straight away in getting into the technical side of paranormal research, as I had a good knowledge of the kind of equipment used from my regular job, where I have daily dealings with all kinds of recording equipment and infrared lighting.

———————

Two locations remain firmly lodged in my memory, and I think they always will. The first was Marwell Hall in Hampshire. It was during a Halloween investigation event that was being hosted by our team for the staff who work at the Hall. I was team leader, and we were in the attic part of the building. This part of Marwell used to be the old servants' quarters and nursery. Unlike the rest of the house, this has been left mostly untouched since it was last used in the early 1900s. Although the rooms have been stripped of furniture, the walls are still decorated as they were when it was an operational part of the house. Our team sat in one of the old rooms and for some time had been hearing footsteps on the bare floorboards in the hall. I said, "If you're out there, can you say hello?" A few seconds later a small voice came back with, "Hello"; the whole team heard it. Other members of the team also heard other disembodied voices in these rooms.

The second experience was in the tunnels at Fort Widley in Portsmouth, Hampshire. I was with three team members and stood about a hundred feet from the entrance to the tunnel. The entry area was lit up, due to the fact it was now used as a fire escape. I thought I saw movement in the lit area at the start of the tunnel. The other team members turned to look, and as we did we all saw the silhouette of an upper torso. It appeared to be shadow-like due to the fact we stood in darkness looking toward light. I ran up the tunnel toward the figure, but as I started running it disappeared. I made it to the fire escape stairs, and one of my fellow team members thought they heard footsteps on the old stairs. I ran up the spiral staircase that led to the surface (around forty feet above us). I reached the top landing and found a fire door. The only way the door opened was out; there was no handle on the outer part of the door, so it was impossible for anyone to have come in that way.

———————

JILL BRUENER — PSYCHIC, MEDIUM, CLAIRVOYANT, AND SPIRITUAL ADVISOR

I have been interested in the paranormal for as long as I can remember. My favourite book in grade school was *The Thing at the Foot of the Bed, and Other Scary Tales*. Ever since I was a child (born in 1953) I have seen spirits and ghosts. I am clairvoyant, which means I see pictures, objects, people, and scenarios vividly in my head. I am also clairaudient, which means I hear answers come to me. If someone asks me a question I will sit for a moment and maybe see a flash of something or hear an answer. I work from voice vibration.

I have been a professional psychic reader for over twenty years, and own Angelspeak Psychic Readings in northern Kentucky, where I have been a lifelong resident. I specialize in psychometry, which is the ability to hold a photograph and read the energy off of the picture. I also specialize in ghosts and hauntings. I taught classes at Northern Kentucky Community College on ghosts and hauntings, and have given countless lectures on the subject.

I am able to walk into any structure, old or new, and tell if there is paranormal activity. I will usually "see" or "hear" the person(s) and be able to tell who they are and why they are there, and, if needed, help them cross over. It may be a haunting, a visitation, or just imprint energy. Sometimes it is the land that is affecting a situation.

I am currently a member of Paranormal Investigators of Northern Kentucky, as their spiritual and psychic advisor. If I am unable to go out on an investigation, the team simply emails me a photo and I am able to remote view the setting and give them my psychic impressions. I was rigorously tested by the team leader and had about 95 percent accuracy when he handed me random photos of previous investigations. My thoughts would correspond to what the home owners' complaints were, right down to smelling cigar smoke and that the house was once occupied by a judge, just by looking at a picture of a stairwell.

I was a weekly guest for over ten years on two of Cincinnati's top morning shows, with listeners calling in asking psychic questions.

Most people can't use the words *psychic* and *Christian* in the same sentence. I can. I love God with all my heart, and I try to serve Him daily. I have dedicated my life to Him and asked for Him to use me as His vessel. I am like a Spiritualist tossed salad with a sprinkling of Christian, Native American, and pagan beliefs tossed in.

I believe God gives us each our own unique gift, and I cherish mine. When I connect with a loved one on the other side I hear them talking to me and telling me information. Sometimes I will get a glimpse of them or others that step in and join them when they come through.

I am a simple person with simple needs. As long as my two sons, my granddaughter, and my best friend, Steve, are healthy and well I am truly blessed.

I have had a lifetime of experiences with the paranormal and continue to do so.

———

A very pretty, petite woman came into my office. She was hoping to connect with her nephew, who had been killed in a car accident when he was only twenty-one. This was such a sad story. This young man had been out drinking with his buddies, and he had driven to a friend's house. He decided he was too intoxicated to drive and made the smart decision to just spend the night where he was. The two friends who rode with him decided they wanted to leave. So they actually picked this young man up and threw him in the back of his car and started to drive home.

Needless to say, they had an accident, and the young man, whom I will refer to as B, was killed instantly. The driver did not have a scratch on him, and the other kid was injured but recovered.

B's family was still grief-stricken at his passing, and his aunt just had to know he was all right. As we began the session, B came in loud and clear. He was so excited to connect with his family.

He told his aunt he was wonderful, and he had a few dos and don'ts he wanted to pass along to his family. His "don't" list included: "Don't visit the crash site anymore, don't go to the cemetery all the time, and don't avoid going places just because I liked to go there." They were actually avoiding restaurants and places he liked to go because they felt guilty that they could be there and B could not. He assured them he could go any place he wanted.

His "to do" request was touching. His father had been a recovering alcoholic who had been clean and sober for the past two years that B was alive. After the accident his father began drinking again. B pleaded with his aunt to talk to his dad and to tell him he was disappointed that he had started drinking again. He reminded her that he wound up dead because of alcohol.

About a week later the aunt made another appointment, and she wanted to bring B's sister to see me. She was a beautiful, sweet girl who was so troubled by her brother's passing that she just could not get on with her life.

This is the incredible part that I would love to share with the world. Their appointment was for noon that day. I went into my reading room to straighten up a bit about 11:30 a.m. I sit at an antique oak table, and I have a white tablecloth on the table. I sat at the table and placed a few pens back in my pen holder and got a fresh notepad out. I then decided the tablecloth was crooked and thought I would straighten it out. I pulled it over to one side and smoothed it out with my hand. Everything was in order, and I walked out of the room.

My secretary, Dawn, had just arrived and I was sitting there chatting with her. Being the great assistant that she is, she always checks my table and makes sure things are in order, as I can be disorganized at times. While I went to answer the door she stepped into my office to make sure everything was in order. B's aunt and sister arrived, and Dawn and I sat and chatted with them for a moment. I then escorted them into my office. I directed them to sit in two chairs, and walked around them to sit in my chair.

I got seated and looked over at them, and the aunt exclaimed, "Look! There's a penny! Jill, did you leave this penny here or put it here for a reason?"

I looked over, and sure enough there was a penny on the table. I was somewhat dumbfounded because I had just smoothed out that white tablecloth a few minutes earlier and there was no penny there. I assured her I had not placed a penny there and that it was not there a few moments ago.

She just looked at me and said, "Oh my God, we were just talking about pennies on the way over here." Someone had sent them an e-mail with a poem about pennies from Heaven. She said she had printed out the poem and added artwork to it and had placed it on B's bed. She and B's sister had been talking about the penny poem in the car and had been wondering if B had seen it.

Well, I can only assume that he had and that he had left the penny there. His sister then picked up the penny and looked at it.

Her hand flew to her mouth, and she said, "Dear God, you will never guess what the date is on this penny."

It was 1979, the year of B's birth. They both started to cry, and I was just dumbstruck. I would have sworn on a stack of Bibles that day that that penny was not on my table before they arrived, and to this day I will still swear an oath to God that there was no penny on that table when I walked out of that room earlier. I am not quite sure how that penny materialized that day on the table, but I am convinced, as is B's family, that he somehow placed that penny there.

When we walked out of my office, we just had to share the story with Dawn. That is when she told me that she had poked her head into my office to make sure everything was in order. She said there was no penny on the table. You may have to place a penny on a white tablecloth yourself to see just how noticeable it would be.

This was one of the most profound and spirit-connected days I have ever experienced. B even made mention of the fact that someone carries something of his in their bra. Well, it turned out that his mother wore a sports bra, and she carried his picture in a small inside pocket of the bra.

He also brought up the fact that he was not happy with the idea of his sister dating one of his friends. He did not approve at all! She acknowledged that her boyfriend said that B had told him on more than one occasion to stay away from his sister.

B then showed me beautiful ribbons suspended in mid-air. I could not quite pick up what he was trying to show me. So I said, "He is showing me these ribbons that just seem to float in the air." They giggled and said they knew what he was trying to say. About four days prior to their visit it was his birthday, and they had released balloons tied with colourful ribbons in honour of him. He also showed me a black-and-white checkered flag and said that someone had placed one on his grave. They acknowledged that they had visited the Kentucky Speedway and that someone had bought a small flag and placed it on his grave.

B begged his family to move on. He said he was happy on the other side and that he was always around them. He encouraged them to stop mourning and grieving. He was trying to give them comfort. He was such a strong spiritual energy, and he came through so easily that they just had to know that he was all right on the other side.

His sister tucked the penny away into her purse, and they actually left smiling. That is such a wonderful feeling to see someone leave with a light heart when they came in so downtrodden over the death of a loved one. B assured them that he was always around and that he loved them.

It does my heart good to know that I am just the messenger.

———————

A mother came to see me who had lost her son. She handed me his picture. As I studied the picture I was looking at a healthy, happy, beautiful little boy. His energy was soft and sweet, and I could tell that while he was here he had been a delightful little soul and had touched many lives.

As I gazed at the photograph, I began to feel his presence coming through. I was just about to tell his mother that her son was here and that he just reached over and kissed her on the cheek when her hand flew up to her cheek.

"Oh God! He is here! I can feel him! I can smell him! My baby! My baby!" she cried.

She was weeping tears of joy, and I have to admit that when I saw her reaction to communicating with her son I had to weep too. It was a very emotional time for all of us. He was trying to comfort his mother and assure her that he was fine.

"I played baseball today with the kids in Heaven, and Grandpa was there on the bench cheering me on! I had a great day today, Mom," he told her.

When she finally got her composure she said that her son had been an all-star baseball player before he became ill. He was showing me that he had developed cancer and that he had become quite ill. He had gone through chemotherapy, but it didn't work. He had lost all his beautiful blond hair and he always wore his blue baseball cap.

He asked me to mention his blue cap to his mom. I am just the messenger, so I told her that her son wanted me to mention his blue hat to her. She let out a gentle sigh, and fumbled through her purse. Then she readily produced an old, worn blue cap.

"This was his favourite cap. I carry it with me all the time. It makes me feel closer to him." She held the old, faded cap gently to her face and inhaled. "I can still smell him, his essence. I just find his cap so reassuring and comforting."

It is not unusual for a loved one to carry a possession of one who has crossed over.

The son assured his mother that he was fine and that he was always around her. Somehow she found strength and comfort in his words, and she told me that she now had a sense of well-being and peace, knowing that her son was all right. When the session was over we shared a hug, and she thanked me for giving her the gift of communicating with her son.

"Always thank God," I told her. "I am just the messenger."

———

A bereaved daughter came to see me when her mother had passed away. Her mother had a massive heart attack and had died en route to the hospital. The daughter felt guilty because she thought that she hadn't done enough for her mother and that the rescue unit was not in time to save her.

I always feel so sorry for people who blame themselves for the death of a loved one. Like they could offset God's plan to call someone home to Heaven by their actions. I try to explain to them that when it is your appointed time and hour, no matter what measures may be taken to save your life you are destined to cross over then. So please, rest assured that if you had to take care of an ailing loved one, you did the best you could and the rest was in God's hands.

Things were going well in the reading. Mom did come through and had several things to say to her daughter. Then Mom kept showing me pearls.

"Ask her about the pearls. It's important! Mention the pearls!"

Sometimes the other side will show you a picture or an image of something, but you are not sure what the significance is. I looked at the daughter and told her that I did not know what Mom was trying to convey, but that she insisted that I bring up the subject of the pearls.

With that, the daughter just broke down. She leaned over and picked up her purse off the floor. She opened her purse and withdrew a small blue velvet bag. She opened the drawstrings of the blue bag and pulled out a pearl necklace. "I always carry these with me wherever I go. My mother was wearing them when she died, and I took them off her body when we arrived at the hospital."

She held the pearls between her fingers and wept. "Now I know my mom was really here. There is no way that you could have known about these pearls."

———

Oftentimes people wish to communicate with a loved one on the other side who is reluctant to come through, or if they do decide to come through they will just linger and don't really want to speak. I find this to be true in some cases where people have committed suicide. They are afraid to connect with their loved ones because of the shame or embarrassment they have caused their family. Even though these people are fine and happy on the other side, it is because of their love of the ones they left behind that they are reluctant to have to face them.

I read for a woman who asked me to contact her brother. She said he had died at the age of twenty-six. He came through and stood by us, but he was not coming in clearly. I did not think that he was a suicide victim, but for whatever reason he was worried that his sister was disappointed with him or that she would judge him. Then he revealed to me that he had died of AIDS. Up until his final days his family had not known that he was ill, and he had never revealed the fact to them that he was gay, although they had their suspicions.

I encouraged him to step forward and talk with his sister. She had indicated that she loved him and that she held no animosity toward him and did not judge him. His reply was that he knew that their mother was crushed and his father was devastated when they found out that their son was gay, because of their religious background.

How unfortunate for this family that because of some organized religion they turned their back on their only son and resented him for who he was. I have two sons, and there is nothing under God's sun that would ever cause me to turn my back on my children. They are precious gifts from God, and they chose us to be their parents. How in the world could one turn one's back on one's own child? This is one question I will never have an answer for.

He talked about how he had always known that he was gay since he was a child and how he had tried to hide the truth from his family. He had moved away as soon as he got out of school to try to hide his lifestyle. The family didn't have too much contact with him. He had not told them that he had AIDS until he had become very ill. He wanted his sister to tell their mother that he was fine and that he heard her talking to him. He was unhappy that he and his father had not made peace before he crossed over. He said that it was Dad's lesson in this lifetime to learn not to judge anyone. His sister wept gently as he talked about old times and growing up and how sad his life had been. He was glad that he had passed over and that he was now in a beautiful place with their grandparents and he was happy.

I had recently done a reading for a woman, probably sometime in September. During that reading she had inquired as to her mother's health, as her mother had cancer. I could sense that her mother would not be around much longer, maybe a few months. I didn't put a time limit on it for her, but I told her that as she well knew her mother would be crossing over soon. Then I told her that her mom could be expecting a visit from her parents before she crossed over to let her know that they would be there for her.

When she came back to see me in December of 2000, her mother had just passed away on Thanksgiving Day. She wanted to contact her mother to make sure she was all right, and she relayed an interesting story to me. She asked if I remembered saying that her mom would be getting a visit from her parents. I acknowledged that I did remember.

The woman then went on, "Well, I went out to the mailbox one day and I checked the mail. There among the bills was a postcard dated 1956. It was a card from Paris, France, from my mom's mother and father. The card read: 'Having a wonderful time, we miss you and we'll see you soon! Love, Mom and Dad.'"

Boy, if that isn't a message from Heaven, I don't know what is!

———

I had a phone call from a woman who asked me if she could come in for a reading as soon as possible. She sounded quite upset, so we agreed she could come in the next day. As soon as she sat down I felt like she wasn't alone and that she had brought in a spirit with her. She sat down across from me and looked at me and then asked if she had any spirits around her. I acknowledged she did, and described the person.

Well, let me back up here a moment. Her boyfriend drove her over to my office and dropped her off. I took an instant dislike to him. I was glad that he just dropped her off and left and would be coming back later to pick her up. I did not want him sitting in my waiting room with my secretary, as she had rolled her eyes at me, signalling to me that she didn't like him either. We will call him Leo.

I will call this young woman Sylvia. She was dark-haired and fair-skinned and a very pretty woman. When I described whom I saw around her she knew instantly who it was. She identified the spirit as Jennifer, the ex-wife of her boyfriend, who had died about a year earlier.

"Yes, she is acknowledging that is who she is, and she is making me feel quite dizzy or out of it. She is showing me that she did not pass from natural causes, but that she died of a drug overdose. Do you understand this?" I asked her.

Sylvia nodded her head in agreement.

"And another thing, she wanted to tell you she did not commit suicide and she did not administer a lethal dose to herself by mistake. She is showing me that someone else was present with her and actually injected her with something. It is a man. She is almost passed out from drugs and alcohol on a couch and she barely wakes up when she feels a tiny needle prick her arm. Then she has the feeling of floating around and out of her body; do you understand this?"

Sylvia told me that no, she did not understand this, and that Jennifer had died from an overdose of morphine, but that by all accounts she had taken an overdose.

"She is almost screaming at me that she did not kill herself and that she knew the exact dosage she could ingest. She is telling me she had help. She said she sees a man bending over her but can't tell who it is, it is dark. But she is screaming at me, 'I didn't kill myself!' She also brings up the point that her death was not reported for some time. Her body was allowed to lay there for a long time even though someone knew she was lying there. She is wondering why he didn't call the police or the ambulance. He knew she was still alive, but he did nothing. He was just pacing, pacing up and down. She said it was a good twelve hours after she actually died that he called for help."

Sylvia acknowledged that Leo had found Jennifer dead, and that yes, she had been quite dead when he found her. Sylvia told me that the very first time she had gone to Leo's house and walked upstairs that she felt like someone was screaming at her to get out of the house. She said the feeling was so severe that she just sat on the floor and thought she was going to be sick. "I didn't feel like this person was mad at me for being there. They just wanted me out of the house, like they were trying to warn me to run away. I felt like I just had to get up off the floor and run out the front door. It was a strange feeling, and somehow I knew it was Jennifer."

"Yes, Jennifer is acknowledging it was her. Believe it or not, she likes you, Sylvia. She thinks you're a great person, and she is afraid for you. She says to tell you that Leo is mean and cruel and can be quite controlling and he's violent. She is afraid for you and wants you to get away from him. She is trying to warn you about him. She said she knows it was him that injected her in the arm with something, but she couldn't see his face. She also says that Leo is the one that got her started on drugs. She thinks he killed her because she was going to leave him, and he would have lost his entire business had they gone through a divorce."

Sylvia just sat there shaking her head. "It's true; he would probably have lost everything if they had gotten a divorce. I know I should get away from him. I have been feeling like I should break up with him. I am just scared."

I affirmed the fact that yes, she should break up with this man as soon as possible and get him totally out of her life. Jennifer was just standing next to me, encouraging me to tell Sylvia to get away from Leo.

"I can only go by what I am shown and what I hear. Jennifer is almost begging you to get away from this man. She says she does not want to see you go through the same heartache and misery she had to endure. She wants you to know she is always around you urging and encouraging you to break off this relationship with Leo. She also wants you to know she is not jealous. She hates him. She does, however, like you, and had the two of you met, she thinks the two of you would have been great friends."

Sylvia sat there in silence for a moment. Then she slowly spoke. "My God, I know she's right. I know I have to get away from Leo. I can just feel that he's changing, and he is becoming more controlling. He wants me to move in with him."

"No!" I shouted at her. Only it wasn't me. It was Jennifer. She had me almost screaming at Sylvia. "Are you out of your mind! Don't do it! Get out while you still can!" The urgency in my voice, via Jennifer, made Sylvia sit up and pay attention.

"I'm calling it off. I'm breaking up with him today." Then she stood up. "Tell Jennifer thank you for me, and she's right, we are good friends already."

I gave her a hug and told her she was doing the right thing. I haven't heard back from Sylvia, but I can only pray that she took Jennifer's advice and got away from Leo.

———

Two sisters came in to see me. They were reluctant because of their religious upbringing and said it was against their religion to seek out a psychic. But they had been encouraged by one whom I will call Martha, because I had placed her in contact with her son many times before and it had given her much comfort.

"Well, if it makes you feel any better I am a licensed Christian minister," I told them. "I only work with God's energy. I believe God gives us each a gift. I think this is mine, and I only use my gift to help people. I am just the messenger."

They were both a little bit nervous, so I explained how I did my readings. They had brought me a picture of their mother, whom they had hoped to be in contact with. Photographs seem to help me connect better with the other side at times. I held their mother's picture, and I could feel her energy as she was waiting to come in and speak with her daughters.

I will call one sister Heather and the other Beth. They were complete opposites. Heather was outgoing and outspoken and very independent. Beth was timid and shy and seemed to be the backbone of the family since Mom's crossing. When Mom came in she described the girls in that manner. She was delighted to see them and acknowledged that she was with her aunt. I described the aunt to them, and they knew exactly who I was talking about. Then they both asked the typical question of did she have anything to tell them, or was she trying to contact them from the other side.

I first looked at Heather and told her that Mom was trying to communicate to her through dreams. She was coming to Heather in the dream state because that is the time when she is still and quiet and Mom can get through to her. She said that Heather was very independent and strong-willed and that it was impossible to get her attention any other way.

Heather acknowledged the fact that she had been having dreams about her mother almost nightly. At that point I had to interject that Heather seemed to have some issues with her mom that she thought she had not cleared up. Heather shook her head and then looked at the floor. I could tell she did not want to elaborate on this subject, so I let it go. I looked over at Beth.

"Mom tells me you are just like her. You are the one who is family-oriented and who has taken over her role. She also acknowledges that you talk to her all the time."

Tearfully Beth nodded her head yes.

"Okay, now I don't know why I see this, it doesn't make sense to me and I get no story or significance with this, but Mom is showing me a teacup and a saucer. That's it. Just an image of a teacup and saucer. Does this make any sense to you, because I don't get it."

Beth put her hand up to her mouth.

"Oh my God! Just last night I was talking to our aunt, and she said that she sometimes feels my mom around and that she has a tiny teacup and saucer that seems to scoot or move, and it has fallen off the table about three or four times. My aunt just laughs and she says hello to my mother. That's wild! So it is my mom doing that. My aunt thought it was her. Yes, that makes perfect sense to me."

Well, I was glad she understood it because I didn't have a clue. Sometimes Spirit will just show you a glimpse of an object or a thought or whatever, and I don't have a clue what they are trying to convey by it. Then I just have to throw it out there and ask: Does this make sense to you?

We continued with the reading, and Mom had several things to tell her daughters. When we were nearing the end of the session I was clearly shown a note or a card in a white envelope. Again, I knew it had something to do with one of the girls, but didn't know which one.

Heather had been extremely quiet and somewhat withdrawn throughout the session, letting Beth do all the talking. I suspected that Heather was one of those people who kept everything bottled up inside and couldn't express her feelings very well.

"Just one more thing before Mom goes. She is acknowledging a card or a note from one of you. She says she appreciates it very much and it was such a heartfelt thing to do, and she thanks you for it immensely."

With that Heather just started sobbing and got up and walked into the bathroom. Beth looked at me and told me that Heather could not express her feelings and emotions in person and that she had left a long letter to her mother on her hospital bed when she left.

The next day their mom died. Mom had just wanted to assure Heather that she had, indeed, read the letter and wanted to tell her daughter thank you for the beautiful words. The girls weren't sure if Mom had read the letter or not.

After Heather regained her composure, she emerged from the bathroom dabbing her eyes. She gave me a big hug and thanked me.

I knew that was hard for her, and probably out of character for her to hug another person, but I also knew in my heart that she knew her mom was all right and that she had read her letter and Heather was able to tell her mom all the things she had wanted to say in person but never could.

I must say the girls had a different outlook on mediumship when they left. They no longer thought it was evil and assured me they would be back.

———

WENDY CALLAWAY — PARANORMAL INVESTIGATOR, SOUTHERN PARANORMAL UK

I am thirty-eight years old, am a qualified accountant, and run my own accountancy practice. I have been attending paranormal investigations now for two years with SPUK after being interested in this area for a number of years. I have had a number of personal experiences, but there are a few that stick in my head.

———

When I was nine I woke up in tears after dreaming that my granddad had died. I woke up upset and wanted my dad, but Mum said he was at Nan's as she had found Granddad dead on the sofa when she came downstairs. This experience has stayed with me, and to this day my parents say it freaked them out.

———

When I was twenty-one my best friend was killed in a car accident. To this day, every time I drive down that stretch of road at night I see him standing in the middle of the road, looking straight at me and smiling. I find it very difficult to forget Chris when he is always there, but because he is smiling I think he is happy, and that gives me some comfort.

———

My aunt was murdered in December 2007; there was a big police investigation, and her ex-husband was the main suspect. My aunt came to me in my room one night and told me that he didn't do it, but he was involved, and that the killer was actually a short, stocky man with dark hair. It turned out that her ex-husband had paid a hit man to kill her who fitted this description exactly. My other aunt also had exactly the same message from my dead aunt on the same night. This is the hardest one to explain for me, as it has been proved to be true through the courts and forensic evidence.

———

LISA CARTER — PARANORMAL INVESTIGATOR, CANADIAN HAUNTING AND PARANORMAL SOCIETY

I am twenty years old and I currently reside in Oshawa, Ontario. I am studying Protection, Security and Investigation, and I personally do not believe in religion.

———

My most memorable experience would have to be at Cornwall Jail in Cornwall, Ontario. While investigating the shower room, I felt a very strong feeling come over me as if two men were loudly yelling in my ear. After further investigation, we discovered an EVP [electronic voice phenomenon] at the same time I experienced that, saying "Die.

———

PETER CLAYTON — STUDENT OF THE SHAMANIC JOURNEY AND AUTHOR

Kundalini is an energy that originates in the lower spinal area of the body and rises up channels in the back, through the various chakra points, until it reaches the upper chakra in the head.

One of the effects of Kundalini is to stimulate the one experiencing it to unusual creative output such as poetry, novels, music composition, etc. My burst of unusual creativity happened after the death of my wife and during the depression I experienced. Suddenly I was writing poetry to a friend, although I had never written poetry before, and it really had some merit. Then I decided to write a novel, *Near Death on Nantucket*, although I had never written fiction before. Again, the novel has been praised by professionals as being a good read, indeed, a page-turner.

I am just an ordinary guy who has had some extraordinary experiences. I was born in Toronto and spent half the year in the city and half the year on Ward's Island. My mother and brother and I lived with my grandparents. As a young child in the summer I would wander the length and breadth of Toronto Islands. Even at the tender age of five or six I would go swimming by myself in Lake Ontario.

It was during such a time that I went into Lake Ontario and almost immediately was over my head and under the water. Strangely, though, instead of being frightening, it seemed so beautiful. I appeared to be surrounded by beautiful, large, many-coloured bubbles, and I felt really comfortable and happy. (It was much later in life, when talking to a psychiatrist friend who had studied the subject of near-death experience, that I was told I had experienced just such an event.)

While enjoying the colours and bubbles I saw a large arm and hand reach down to me. It pulled me out of the water. A man I did not know took me back to the beach, put me down on a towel under an umbrella, told me not to tell my mother what had happened as she was not well and it would worry her, then walked away. I don't remember that there was anyone with me under the umbrella. After a while I got up and went home, and no, I never did tell my mother.

To this day I have no idea who the man was. Given the later events in my life, I think it possible that I might have just had my first angelic intervention in my life. I was to have others.

When I was an adult I married and we had two boys. I worked for many years for advertising agencies, ending up as vice-president and creative director for a large American agency's Canadian branch. Advertising was an exciting occupation. I loved it, and it was kind to me.

I eventually left my advertising career and joined with three colleagues to start a music company. We were quite successful, producing first The Guess Who, a music group that went on to be the biggest act in North America for a while, and then Alice Cooper, who also became the biggest act in North America after The Guess Who had cooled off a little. That was fun. When we sold our studio and business I joined a Molson company, then moved to another Molson company before finally retiring. They were fun, too.

Eventually my wife died and left me wondering if that was all there was. It was shortly thereafter I started to write again, first poetry then a novel. I didn't question it at the time, but though I had never written poetry I began to produce works of some merit. Then I suddenly wanted to write a novel. I had never written in this mode either, and it turned out to be a wonderful and somewhat mysterious process. Those familiar with Kundalini have said that I went through a Kundalini rising but suffered no pain, which is possible with Kundalini rising. The only sign was an elevation in creativity.

I can see or sometimes sense spirits, but this is just a gift for which I am most grateful. What I have had that is considered paranormal begins with my near-death experience when I was a child. Having an NDE is considered to be able to confer paranormal powers on most if not all who experience it. I believe that may be the reason I have experienced the events that I have had for many years.

———

I woke in the night hearing the sound of someone breathing. I turned on the light, but there was nothing visible, and the sound of breathing stopped. I turned off the light and it began again. I listened closely to make sure I wasn't hearing some other sleeper in one of the other bedrooms, but it was clearly in my room.

As I was listening it seemed to touch me, I guess because every nerve in my body got a jolt like a live wire had touched me. I then said to the presence that that was unacceptable and it would have to leave. I have my own means of clearing a room or space if I feel it is necessary for some reason. All the sounds and the explosive nerve jolt stopped at that time and did not start again. I went back to sleep.

———

I have another experience that I never put down to "haunting," but I guess you might classify it as such. A friend and I were returning to her place in Muskoka around midnight. The Muskoka roads are pitch black on a moonless night, and my headlights suddenly illuminated the figure of a young woman standing unmoving at the side of the road, with her hand in an upright position.

The interesting thing was her dress was of a style of the late 1800s. My friend was startled and asked, "What is that young woman doing standing at the side of this road this late at night?" I asked if she could describe the woman's dress. As my friend is an artist, she could describe in great detail the colours and style of dress. And what, I asked, would be the year such a dress might actually be worn? Well, she thought the turn of the century. I told her she had seen a spirit; that bothered her a great deal. I didn't say, but I knew why we had seen the woman.

The next day she suggested we go back over the road in the daylight to pick out the actual place of the sighting. She has lived in the area for many years and was quick to identify the place in the daylight. It was at the driveway of an empty lot. Across the road was a cemetery, so I suggested we go and see if we could find a name and date that might correspond to the turn-of-the-century dress. I am a dowser, and I quickly located a small stone with a woman's name and a date of 1898. She died when she was twenty years old.

I later took the time to ask to have the woman helped home, as it seemed to me that was why she had presented herself to us, and I believe she finally left this level to go where she should have gone those many years ago. I was pleased to have been able to help her.

———

But my experiences go well beyond these sort of normal events (normal to me, anyway). I have been a student of the shamanic journey for many years, and there are wonderful experiences available to the one experiencing the journey. The best one for me was when I was able to rescue my brother, who never properly went home when he died.

While attending a Shamanic Death and Dying workshop, we were encouraged to journey and see if we could find a spirit that needed rescuing. I went to my power animal in spiritual reality and suggested we check out whether my brother, who had died about six months previously, had made a proper transition. We journeyed until we ended up in the room at the hospice where he had died and found him still lying on the bed.

I had just gotten him up and talking to me when my mother came into the room and said, "It's okay. I can take him now."

I returned to ordinary reality, and we all discussed our journeys. When the workshop leader heard mine he was very impressed and suggested I do another journey to see if there was any further work necessary. Again I went to my power animal in spiritual reality and said, "Let's see if Jim has gone home." I might interject here that one must always journey with intent. Again we journeyed until we arrived at a park-like area and began to walk up a path beneath large, leafy trees.

I then heard my mother's voice, although I did not see her this time. She said, "Leave him alone now. He's tired." I smiled and thought, *Once a mother always a mother*, and returned to ordinary reality.

This has always been the most emotional and memorable journey I have ever taken.

———

For some time I had been aware of my brother apparently cohabiting my body. Often when looking in the mirror I would see his face rather than mine. I didn't mind, although I was somewhat surprised to witness this odd occurrence, as it had never happened before. I was sort of channelling my brother, although I have never channelled before and have no interest in the subject except for a lady of my acquaintance who does channelling.

I suppose I should have done something about this peculiar situation, but I didn't really think about it until a most unusual and embarrassing event occurred during a dinner with my wife, my first cousin, and my brother's wife. When we sat down to dinner in a pub in Toronto I was sitting next to my sister-in-law (in whom, incidentally, I have yet to confide about this event in the restaurant) and dear brother took over; I guess I was channelling him.

I became aware that I was staring closely into my sister-in-law's face and stroking her arm. She broke the spell by asking me, in no uncertain terms, to let go of her arm. I suddenly became alert to the situation and stopped the arm-stroking immediately.

Dinner passed without further incident, and later I had time to review what had happened. It was then I realized that my brother had used me to get next to his wife, whom he loved dearly.

I decided once was enough of that and immediately took steps to send him packing. I love my brother, but once was enough for that kind of shenanigans. I had to banish him, although I was sort of sorry to see him leave.

I no longer see his face in the mirror and now have no sense of his presence.

———

BARRI GHAI — PARANORMAL INVESTIGATOR, THE GHOSTFINDER PARANORMAL SOCIETY

I am the founder and lead investigator of the United Kingdom's number-one paranormal investigation society, The Ghostfinder Paranormal Society. I established GPS with my best friend, Ian Wilce, several years ago to try and help more people understand the world of the paranormal and to specifically obtain evidence that ghosts do exist.

I first became interested in ghosts and the supernatural from a very young age after having terrifying experiences at my family home. As a young boy I saw shadows move across the walls of my room, heard my name being whispered when I was alone, and was attacked by a demonic entity after finally confronting the presence alone in my bedroom. I grew up sensing the spirits, and gradually seeing and hearing more, until I learned to turn this gift off and control things for peace of mind.

I think that becoming a ghost hunter was always in the cards for me. I used to be fascinated with everything paranormal and read all the books I could get on the subject. I became particularly interested in ghosts and UFO phenomena as a teenager and decided to join paranormal groups and societies to learn more about the world of paranormal investigations and to actively take part.

It was whilst working for an Internet television network where I was asked to produce a short feature about ghosts and ghost hunting that I truly became inspired to act out my ambitions and turn my keen interest into something more. This desire to begin investigating was postponed slightly after I became a father to my first daughter, and working life took over as a matter of priority.

However, a few short years later my need to explore the mysteries of the paranormal was always just bubbling under the surface, and I continued to research all I could through books, films, and the Internet, before officially launching The Ghostfinder Paranormal Society in 2006.

Most of my life is currently dedicated to the investigation of paranormal phenomena, and when I am not managing the GPS website and team, I am investigating haunted locations across the United Kingdom and helping people who need our advice and guidance.

———

I first came face to face with a human apparition whilst in my third year of university. I saw a young girl aged about seven or eight standing next to my bed. She was wearing a Victorian white frock and seemed very real, but wasn't completely opaque and just stood playing with her hair and smiling at me intently for a few seconds before dissipating into the blackness of the room.

———

During a recent investigation of a famous bar at London's Canary Wharf, I was pulled hard on the back of my jacket, causing me to fall off a coffee table. The experience left me shaken up and a little unsettled for the remainder of the investigation.

———

Tutbury Castle in Staffordshire, England, is one of my favourite haunted locations in England. At the beginning of 2011, my team and I were delivering a public paranormal event to over fifty participants. A group of ten people were being led by myself and another GPS investigator in the South Tower of the castle when we began experiencing high EMF fluctuations, and two members of the group psychically picked up on a child's energy circling us. I called out and asked the spirits to show themselves. I looked up at the tower ruins and briefly caught glimpse of a bluish ball of light pulsate in an abandoned turret above us. Amazingly, this was also seen by several members of the group and was documented as being unexplained and possibly paranormal in origin.

———

When I was about six years old, I remember staying at my cousin's house for the weekend. I was left alone playing in a bedroom upstairs and can recall seeing a blue toy car begin to move across the floor unaided. The toy began to move slowly but then picked up speed before slowing down to a stop around six feet from where it had been positioned on the carpeted floor. There was no logical explanation for this, and I was terrified.

———

Whilst investigating Castle Menzies in the highlands of Scotland live on a UK satellite television channel last Halloween, I was amazed to actually receive direct responses to my questions using the K2 EMF Meter and Gauss Master. The EMF responses were so clear and precise that it truly astonished me. We were without a doubt definitely communicating with a spiritual entity. The only problem was being broadcast live meant it was all cut short, and we were made to move on through to other less interesting areas. I will return to Castle Menzies again to finish the job I started and am convinced we will obtain real, tangible proof that spirits do haunt this amazing, prominent Scottish castle.

DAVE GIBB — PARANORMAL INVESTIGATOR, CANADIAN HAUNTING AND PARANORMAL SOCIETY

I have been investigating now for eighteen years, almost seven since the team's inception. I am also a married father of four girls, and have been a student and teacher of the martial arts for eighteen years. I was raised in Oshawa, Ontario, grew up in the Spiritualist Church, and eventually moved to Pembroke, Ontario, where I founded the team [CHAPS]. I am forty years old. I manage an industrial pipe sales company, now back in Oshawa.

My experiences have been extensive, really, from having flashes of light exploding in my car in Gettysburg, being pushed out of a room, to a coffin lid falling off during an investigation of a mansion.

I would say the latter sticks out in my head as, for one of the first times, I broke my own rule about running and regretted it with a separated shoulder.

JULIE HARWOOD — AUTHOR AND PARANORMAL INVESTIGATOR, SOUTHERN PARANORMAL UK

I am thirty-six years old and live in Poole on the south coast of the United Kingdom. I am an author (*Haunted Poole* and *Haunted Dorchester*) and am currently working on my third book. I am also the founding member and Group Manager of Southern Paranormal UK, a paranormal investigation team. I founded the team in 2005, and we have not looked back since, having investigated some of the UK's apparently most haunted buildings. In 2009 we also became part of The Atlantic Paranormal Society's international family.

————

It was at the Kings Theatre in Southsea that I had my most memorable experience. We were investigating the theatre, and it was my team's time to investigate the auditorium. There were eight of us in the team and so I split us all up. Two people went up "into the Gods" (the upper level seating), I and a guest sat in one box, three other members sat in the box opposite us, and the last member stayed on the ground floor in front of the stage.

After a short while the guest sat next to me looked past me to our right and let out an "Aahhhh" at the top of her voice. I asked what she had seen and looked over to see a man sat in the shadows approximately fifteen feet from us. Kieran, one of the members in the other box, was filming, and Mark, the investigator in front of the stage, quickly took a still picture.

I peered through the dark and then said, "Don't panic, it's just Richard." Richard was one of the members that had gone up to the top-level seating. I presumed he had just come down for some reason and was sitting quietly as to not disturb us.

We all had a giggle, and I leaned forward out of the box and said, "Please don't make my guests jump, Richard." Oddly, he did not answer, but I thought it was because he was embarrassed. He just got up and walked out of the theatre through double doors. As he did this I heard a voice from two levels above us. It was Alison, the other member that was up there with Richard, and she was wondering why we were talking to Richard as he was up there with her and had not moved. Obviously, on hearing that, the team jumped in to action. I immediately radioed the other team, who were sitting behind the double doors (where the unknown man had exited). The entire team confirmed that no one had come through the doors that they had been less than two feet away from.

This man was sighted by eight people, and we have him on recording and in a picture. The theatre was locked down, and so we know no one had come into the theatre. Despite all of this, even if someone had gotten in, we saw him go through doors into an area where no one saw him!

NICKI HIMMELMAN — PARANORMAL INVESTIGATOR, LIGHT WORKERS PARANORMAL INVESTIGATION

"I am a thirty-eight-year-old married mother of three. I have been interested in the paranormal since I was a child. My professional background is community-based facilitation and special education. I like to refer to myself as a skeptical believer, as in I do believe in ghosts, but I am the type of person who hates "fluffy" evidence: things that can be easily explained or doubtful. Seeing/feeling/hearing is believing!

The experience that stands out for me was on my first official investigation. As the team was setting up inside a cave-like structure, I witnessed a shadowy figure pass by the entrance of the cave, not once but twice. At first I brushed it off as my imagination, but the second time one of my teammates witnessed it as well and validated exactly what I had seen. What made it even more remarkable was the fact that it looked like a man, but you could see right through him. He walked in the same direction both times. Our team leader showed us that it could have not been a live person, as the route that he had travelled led right off a cliff.

SCOTT HOBBS — PARANORMAL INVESTIGATOR, THE THUNDER BAY PARANORMAL SOCIETY)

I am a co-founder of the Thunder Bay Paranormal Society, and currently the organization's case manager. A skeptic by nature, I became interested in the paranormal nearly fifteen years ago while witnessing unexplained things at a vacant hospital, working night security.

Despite nearly thirteen years of study and two years of hands-on investigating, I still believe in taking a skeptical approach to every case we receive. Outside of the paranormal investigation world, I work in marketing and communications, and pastimes include travel, camping, playing football, and watching hockey.

————

The place we were investigating was a small bungalow in town. We had already investigated it once and had found some really compelling evidence that something was going on … but it wasn't enough to close the file, so we went back.

That night we heard and saw a few things, but nothing had really convinced me it was going to be an exciting night. About half an hour before we were to wrap up, I and two other investigators were sitting in the basement, wrapping up an EVP session. I was staring out of the room down the hallway when suddenly I clearly saw something darker than the already darkened hallway run from the room on the right side of the hall across and up the stairs.

We went to investigate and found no sign of anything. I thought at first it could have been my eyes playing tricks on me, but we also found a cold spot nearby. A week later the family told us they have often seen very similar shadows.

The audio picked up some really great EVPs that coincided with our experiences.

————

Amanda Horley — Paranormal Investigator, Southern Paranormal UK

I have always had an interest in old buildings and the "feeling" of buildings, spending a lot of time visiting ruins and old houses. Prior to joining the group I had had several experiences that I couldn't explain, the earliest specific one being in my mid-teens.

However, even as a younger child I loved Portchester Castle in Hampshire, and visited it often with my family. I could feel the life within the walls. When given the chance to help investigate a supposedly haunted building on my fortieth birthday, I jumped at the chance. It was a different way to celebrate a milestone age.

That night I saw a figure in one room and had several other experiences as well, including having a torch turned off, hearing footsteps and noises within the building, and feeling that there were other people with us that we couldn't see.

Shortly afterwards I was asked to help out when Southern Paranormal came to investigate this building, and was fascinated by the way they worked. I was asked if I wanted to join the group and realized that this would be a way to learn more about something that I realized held a strong fascination for me.

Since being a member of the group, I have learnt to channel abilities that previously I had little control over. I love both the scientific side of the investigations (and would describe myself as a scientist by nature) and the psychic side of investigations, often sensing presences (and having them verified later), and still to this day get a buzz out of "feeling" a building's emotional attachments.

———

In the last eight or so years that I have been a member of the group Southern Paranormal UK, I have had so many experiences that mean a lot to me for different reasons, as well as having had some strange things happen before I joined the group.

I suppose one that made a really big impact was not actually a sighting, but came awfully close. The group were having a long weekend in Wales and were due to investigate Ruthin Gaol. I had been holidaying on the north Welsh coast, and had to pass through Ruthin to get to the accommodation we were due to stay at.

In almost every investigation we have done, I go in blind, not knowing any of the history. It's how I prefer to work, but that day I decided to visit [Ruthin] Gaol as a tourist. I don't know why, it just seemed the right thing to do at the time. I walked into a cell called the Condemned Man's Cell, where prisoners were held immediately prior to being hung.

Inside was set a tableau of a man in prisoner's uniform, sitting on a bench holding a photo of his family and with his head in his hand. Next to him stood a priest reading from the Bible.

As I walked into the cell, I would swear that the head of the prisoner mannequin turned slightly toward me, and his eyes flicked in my direction. I backed out of the cell very rapidly, startling a man who sat on the landing with his two children.

Although this was unnerving, I did enter the cell again briefly and got the distinct impression that the mannequin was going to stand up. I know that there were no animatronics in these figures.

I continued my journey, and didn't say anything about the incident to my friends when we met up. That night, when we were being taken on a walk round the jail by our host, I deliberately held back at the Condemned Man's Cell, and was delighted when one of the ladies reappeared rapidly from the cell and said that it looked like the mannequin had moved.

We then split into our teams for the vigils, and I couldn't wait to go back to that area. I let my teammates go into the cell before me, and even as I followed them in I could see the eyes moving to watch us. There were three of us in the cell, and the other lady in the group had not experienced the "moving" mannequin in the earlier walk around, but was certainly aware of him now.

As we stood there I could see the rise and fall of the man's back, and was very aware of the eyes watching us. I and the other lady were both unnerved by what was happening, and holding hands (very brave) we slowly approached the mannequin and touched it.

As expected, it was hard and unyielding to the touch. However, despite the fact that I still felt that the man was about to stand up, and he was certainly very aware of our close proximity, I wanted to put my arm around his shoulders and comfort him.

I returned later in the evening with another member of the group, who had been in a different vigil team and was unaware of our experiences. I asked him to walk into the cell, and he did, although he backed out again immediately, pointing at the mannequin and asking me if it had moved.

We cannot explain what happened, and my own personal view is that by chance, the mannequin happened to occupy a space where a condemned man *did* sit prior to his sentence being carried out. The energy present gave the impression that the mannequin was moving. For me, the fact that it first happened when I wasn't trying to pick up on energies, together with watching my friends all experience similar things, was fascinating.

Initially it was almost frightening, but after having plucked up the courage to touch the mannequin, I felt very sorry for the man and wanted to comfort him. Still can't really decide why that happened, as although touching the mannequin proved it was harmless, it still felt like it was going to stand up. I just wasn't frightened of it anymore.

———

MARIE HOLDER — PARANORMAL INVESTIGATOR, SOUTHERN PARANORMAL UK

I have been with the group for about five and a half years and am Report Co-ordinator. I've had an interest in the paranormal since I was around six years old and have always been fascinated by ghosts and loved walking round cemeteries and reading the inscriptions on the gravestones. I have a number of books on the subject, my favourite being *The World's Greatest Ghosts*.

———

My most memorable experience whilst with the group was during an investigation in Old Portsmouth. Our team was doing a glass divination, and the glass was really responding to our questions.

When [the spirits were] asked to do something else to show that they were in the room, I felt extremely cold all of a sudden, as if I'd been shut in a freezer.

The feeling was really intense, and I felt as if they were right behind me. I thanked them for this, and the feeling subsided.

———

JAMIE JACKSON — PARANORMAL INVESTIGATOR, GETTYSBURG GHOSTS

I have been interested in the paranormal since I was little, maybe about five years old. My family used to tell my cousin and me ghost stories, real and fictitious, when we were just tiny kids. When I was a little older I borrowed true ghost story books from the library and scared myself silly. Gettysburg Ghosts came about because of my interest in the Civil War and the paranormal. The website was created in 2000. I live only fifteen minutes from the battlefield, so it makes it convenient to investigate the area.

———

The most memorable experience I've had was really three separate events that as a whole were quite scary. One summer evening, my family and I and a couple of fellow investigators went to Spangler Spring in Gettysburg. My mom and sister walked toward an area where large boulders were scattered amongst some trees. My mother was asking my sister something, and she did not respond. My mom looked at her, and she was staring straight ahead looking at nothing. My mom had to shout her name several times and shake her before my sister responded by saying, "I'm so cold," after which she began sobbing uncontrollably. It was spooky at the time, but I thought nothing of it.

Two months later we were once again at the Spring; this time my brother and a friend were along in addition to the rest of my family and some friends. It was an active night. We smelled sulphur (burnt gunpowder) and saw lights in the woods. We had some blood-curdling EVPs of a hideous screeching noise as well. While listening to EVPs standing amongst the boulders and trees, I noticed my brother was shaking and sniffing. He started pacing and then burst into tears and sobbed uncontrollably.

He kept saying, "I'm going to die. I'm going to die." And then he would say, "I know I'm not dying, but I feel like I have to say, 'I'm going to die.'"

He couldn't stop crying. Now I was a bit nervous. My brother is not emotional; he hates even hugging, let alone crying in front of a group of people. Still, I wasn't convinced and told my cousin, "I won't completely believe it unless it happens to me."

Two weeks later at the Spring, we had another active night. I heard people whispering in my ear and thought people were playing pranks on me. At one point, we all were looking at a bright white light (the lady in white frequents this area). My brother was nervous and told everyone not to look at the light, that it did not want us there, and we should leave. Another member of the group said something, and I turned to look at him. Over his shoulder was a face, clear as could be, of a man or boy.

At that moment, I reached out to this gentleman and said, "We need to leave," at which time I started sobbing uncontrollably. I couldn't stop, and I felt like someone needed me, but I couldn't help them.

I remember saying through my tears, "This is so cool!"

We left the area. Later I mentioned to my mother how I had seen a face, and I described it as being clean-shaven or young and with sandy blond hair, very tall and thin. My mother looked at me with surprise and explained that two weeks earlier my sister had also seen someone behind my brother before he started crying. At first she thought it was my brother's friend, but his friend walked over from the opposite direction. The man my sister saw was also tall, thin, clean-shaven with light brown hair.

A humorous experience, though, was at the Triangular Field in Gettysburg. A group of us were walking up the hill, leaving. I was in the back of the line, and I said, "Wait, I don't want to be in back because something might grab me."

I ran ahead to the front of the group. About four to five minutes later, I screamed bloody murder. Something had grabbed my biceps and held me. I felt my jacket being pushed against my stomach, as if I had walked into someone and they grabbed me to keep from falling. I went to the back of the line after that.

The most spiritually uplifting experience I had was in Gettysburg while taking EVP recordings. I got a recording that was quite clear. It said, "Help me; help me, please."

It sounded so sad that I started to cry. I told the spirit that he only had to ask for help and he would receive it. After I said that there was a flash of light that shot across the field I was in.

On my recorder you hear me tell the spirit to ask for help. You hear a garbled voice scream for help, then you hear me say, "What was that? I just saw a light shoot across there!"

I believe that what I witnessed was a spirit making it toward the light.

KIMBERLEY LAPIERRE — PARANORMAL INVESTIGATOR, LIGHT WORKERS PARANORMAL INVESTIGATION

My interest in the paranormal began at a very early age. I'm originally from Rockland, Ontario (just outside Ottawa), and my earliest experiences occurred in the 150-year-old renovated log house I moved into when I was eleven years old. As a young skeptic, I attributed most of my early experiences to an overactive imagination cultivated in a time-worn setting, but as I got older I realized that maybe I should not have brushed off those earlier experiences.

In March of 1997, I moved to Halifax, Nova Scotia, with my husband, and things just intensified from that point on. For my first two years in Halifax, we lived in an apartment complex just off the Bedford Highway, where both my husband and I experienced paranormal occurrences. While we didn't share our experiences with a lot of people, family and close friends were aware of the activity that was occurring in our apartment while we were living there.

After two years of "spirited" apartment living, we bought a house and moved to Timberlea. We both thought that the events of the previous two years would be behind us, but it wasn't long before things started up in our new home as well. At first, I was the only one to witness the strange occurrences that went on in the house, but by the time our oldest daughter was eighteen months old and able to verbalize well, she started to share her experiences as well. Our children are now thirteen and ten and they have each had experiences that have moulded them in one way or another.

I appeared on the show Ghostly Encounters in the fall of 2010 to share some of my experiences. While nothing harmful has ever happened in my home, my youngest daughter has been frightened by the sighting of the ghost of an old woman. This particular spirit has also been seen by myself and my husband on two separate occasions.

I lead Light Workers Paranormal Investigation in Halifax, Nova Scotia, and my team's sole purpose is to help people who are experiencing activity and to gather evidence of paranormal activity. We don't try to debunk claims, but we do look for other possible and plausible explanations in the course of our investigations.

———

Although I have seen, heard, felt, and even smelled some amazing things on our investigations, my most memorable experience occurred in my own home and was one of the stories featured on Ghostly Encounters. My oldest daughter, Reilly, had just turned two, and we had given her two cellophane helium-filled balloons for her birthday. One of the balloons was a big yellow happy face, but I can't recall what the other one was. They each had about three or four feet of coiled ribbons hanging off of them, and we were having a blast playing in the basement.

My daughter would yank on the ribbons to get the balloons to come down, then she would let them go and giggle as they hit the ceiling again. When it was time for bed I told her the balloons had to stay in the basement because I was concerned the ribbons might become tangled around her neck if she took them to bed with her. Being two, she had a complete meltdown and had to be carried upstairs to bed, kicking and screaming the whole time as she cried out for her balloons. She finally fell asleep after about an hour of carrying on, and I wasn't far behind her.

The next morning when I opened my eyes the first thing I saw was happy face balloon smiling at me as it floated midway between ceiling and floor directly in front of her closed bedroom door. I jumped out of bed and, grabbing the balloon by the ribbons, gave it a yank and let it go. The balloon floated all the way up to the ceiling and stayed there.

I live in a semi-detached split entry house, and there is no possible way that the balloon could have travelled to where it ended up all on its own. It would have had to cross the playroom in the basement, drop two feet to go through the doorway, turn right to go up the stairs, turn right at the landing, turn left at the living room, cross the living room on the main floor, turn right to go up the stairs to the second floor, then make another right at the top of the stairs to end up in front of my daughters' room. I also don't have an explanation as to why it was floating midway between ceiling and floor. My only guess is that someone wanted her to have her balloon. This was just one of the many experiences I've had in my house over the years.

———

The most amazing thing about [the balloon] experience was that it occurred shortly after another unexplainable experience with the same daughter. She was being toilet trained at the time, so when she awoke in the middle of the night, I led her to the bathroom and placed her on the toilet while I took a seat on the side of the tub. While she was sitting there she looked me right in the eyes and calmly said, "I'm not afraid, Mommy." I was confused, and admittedly a little scared, by the way she spoke the words. I reluctantly asked her why she would be scared. She told me that when she woke up, Grandma was sitting on the edge of her bed, but that she had told her not to be scared, so she wasn't.

I was a little unnerved by our middle-of-the-night conversation and quickly tucked her back into bed and went back to sleep myself. The next morning we received a 6:00 a.m. call from my husbands' parents to inform us that his grandmother, who was 103, had passed away during the night. Her time of death coincided with our daughter's nighttime visit.

I've always felt that she was the one that brought Reilly her balloon in the middle of the night.

———

IAN MURPHY — LEAD INVESTIGATOR, PARANORMAL RESEARCH ASSOCIATION OF BOSTON

I am originally from Ireland, and before forming the Boston team I was the founder of the Paranormal Research Association of Ireland. The Irish team is still going strong under the leadership of my previous deputy lead investigator, David Wegner (ironically, from Boston).

The Paranormal Research Association of Boston is a team of scientific paranormal researchers coming from all walks of life. We are dedicated to the research of all claimed paranormal experiences, with a threefold mission:

1. Above all, to help people who are suffering from paranormal experiences in their residences / places of work.
2. To further our, and as a consequence the public at large's, understanding of paranormal activity through logical, verifiable scientific means.
3. Through presentations, classes, and our published research papers, to give the public an understanding of both paranormal activity and the methods we use to locate and test paranormal activity.

We use tried and tested methods along with cutting-edge technology/ theory, developed in-house and from the community, to further our knowledge and research techniques. In turn, this enhances the service we give to our clients.

———

I have had many memorable experiences in my time as a paranormal investigator, from finding anomalies on video and audio files to strange feelings and tricks of the light I've seen with my own eyes.

But I think my most memorable experiences are with my clients. I have had two such clients that always stick in my mind. One was a client from a number of years ago. She believed she was being attacked by a spirit every night for a number of weeks.

We had a long discussion, including a concise history, and with her history of stress, moving, and insomnia we found she had a condition known as sleep paralysis, which is closely related to REM atonia. With a name for her condition, and the client information sheet, she was able to get rid of the "ghost."

Another example that comes to mind is a young couple who had just moved into a new home. They had classic haunting phenomena: electronics turning on and off, headaches, feelings of being watched.

The couple had already moved from their home because of the disturbances. After an extensive survey, we found the problem was with the electrical system. After a brief visit from the electrician, we solved the problem and the couple were able to move back in.

Dr. Dave Oester — Co-founder of International Ghost Hunters Society with Dr. Sharon Oester

I grew up in an old haunted farmhouse and learned that ghosts were a part of the experiences of the living. I have been active in this field for many years.

In December 1990, we started looking for a place along the Oregon coast to move to, and in January 1991 we relocated to the Oregon coast and rented a haunted cottage. It was here that we learned to live with playful spirits, and this experience became the motivation for us to begin our writing careers in the paranormal.

We quickly researched how ghost research was being done in the UK and applied my background in physics, electronics, and photography to develop a method for conducting ghost investigations.

I realized early on that most ghost hunters followed the traditional approach to investigations, which was not effective. We developed standards and protocols for conducting field investigations that was based on the scientific approach, without using mediums or psychics.

In 1998 we offered the first home-study course for becoming a ghost hunter through our website. We introduced ghost photography to the Internet and became the leading movement for ghost hunting on the Web.

———

I was in Kings Cemetery in Oregon. It was about dusk, the moon had not yet come up, but the fog was rolling into the cemetery. The cemetery was not maintained well, and the graves of the Native Americans who were killed fighting the white settlers were not kept up at all. I had walked into that section and was taking photos and suddenly I felt the psychological presence of a spirit who did not want me to be there.

I could feel my hair stand up, a cold chill ran down my spine, but I refused to depart until I had taken the last of my photos. When I was done, I was thinking about all those scenes in films where the car would not start as the creature slowly descended upon its victim. I did not run because my legs were too weak, but I made it back to the car and it did start and I was able to drive out without incident.

———

I can remember another time we were investigating a cemetery in Douglas, Wyoming, late one night. The full moon was out and it was kind of spooky. We were walking along the grave edge of the children's section when my foot slipped off the grass and into the loose dirt. My shoe sank down to my ankles and I screamed. My scream scared Sharon, so she screamed, and then I screamed again, thinking that the spirit had her also. I still remember thinking this was dumb, but the Hollywood versions of a hand coming out of the grave and grabbing my ankle still lurked in my mind.

———

I remember working with a person who had lost her only child. She was grieving and out of sorts with herself and her life. She had some experiences and did not know how to deal with those experiences. I explained that love does go beyond the grave and our loved ones are not far from us even in death. They may not dwell with us, but they do return often to make sure we are okay. They are okay and want us to get on with our lives and not grieve for them because they are happy and well.

When I explained some of the events that could happen that were from the spirits, she immediately recognized her own experiences and realized it was her son letting her know he was okay and that she should not grieve for him. I simply shared what we had learned over the dozen years we have been ghost hunting and it helped this woman to accept that her son still loved her and wanted her to get on with her life.

———

SARAH PETTET — PARANORMAL INVESTIGATOR AND SENIOR TRAINER, SOUTHERN PARANORMAL UK

I am a paranormal investigator and senior trainer for Southern Paranormal UK in my spare time. I collaborate with Southern Paranormal UK's founder and Team Manager, Julie Harwood, to develop and run training sessions for the team, from new member training to team-leading.

I joined Southern Paranormal in 2006, with my sister; we had been looking at joining a group, and Southern Paranormal UK came across as the most professional and together group there was in our region.

I have always had an interest in the paranormal ever since childhood. I cannot put a finger on exactly why, or what drew me toward the paranormal, only that I cannot remember a time when the interest wasn't there.

I have always been aware that I have been sensitive to things, kind of an empathy/clairsentient, and I have found working with the team has allowed this ability to grow and develop more.

However, I do not totally accept everything as being paranormal; I will try to look for a normal solution for any apparent phenomena.

———

As a child I remember sitting with my nephew at the top of our stairs, in a relatively dark, windowless hallway, watching all these pretty white lights moving at varying speeds around us.

———

Within the group I would say one my best experiences was one of those double-take experiences in an old RAF hangar, where I saw an apparition in full Second World War flying gear behind me whilst taking some photos during an investigation. Initially I sensed someone stood behind me and thought it was a member of the vigil team, so I quickly glanced, and it wasn't till I turned back around that I registered what I had seen. Of course, when I looked back he had gone.

———

There are several times when I have sensed a spirit around me on an investigation and the team have noted my physical appearance seems to have changed. There have been times when we have experienced the atmosphere in a room change and affect us all in some manner; the most memorable of these made us feel a bit giggly and silly like we were under the influence of alcohol (and we definitely had not touched a drop!) in one room, yet on the next vigil in another room we were very sombre and serious.

———

Another experience happened just recently, when, whilst sitting on a bench in a room with another team member, we felt something physically brush past our legs. We looked for an explanation — if it had been an animal it would still have had to have been in the location as there was no way for anything to get out or hide — and found none!"

———

LYNSEY ROBSON — PHOTOGRAPHER AND PARANORMAL INVESTIGATOR, LIGHT WORKERS PARANORMAL INVESTIGATION

I have had an interest in the paranormal from a very young age. Being a curious person, I've always found anything unknown to be intriguing. I had an experience when I was a young child; however, at the time,

I didn't understand what it was I was experiencing. I've always had a keen interest in history, and was very fortunate to travel the world with my parents when growing up. I believe this enhanced my thirst for knowledge and for answers to the harder questions in life, including "What happens after death?"

———

When I was about three years old, I would often wake up in the night. It was something that bothered my parents to no end. They'd pick me up from wherever in the house I'd wandered around to, plunk me back into bed, and hope that I'd stay there for the rest of the evening.

I remember fairly clearly why I woke up each night. There was a sound that would wake me up. I would lie in my bed and hear this familiar sound. At first I had no idea what it was, but it sounded familiar. So I'd hobble out of bed and wander downstairs in search of the source.

I don't recall how long it took me to find the source of the sound, but I remember coming around the corner into our old living room and seeing our wooden rocking chair moving back and forth. I knew immediately that the source of the sound was the chair.

It didn't seem at all odd to me that there was an older woman in a long dress sitting in the chair and rocking back and forth. My parents told me that eventually they'd find me sitting in front of the chair, talking. When I claimed I was talking to the woman, they took it as just a flight of childhood fancy and plunked me back in bed. This experience began it all for me.

———

MARIA STREET — SENIOR CO-ORDINATOR, SOUTHERN PARANORMAL UK

I am forty-five years old, and being born on Halloween (such a cool birthday), you could say I have had a lifetime interest in the paranormal. I also had a very loving granddad who loved to sit me on his knee and tell me ghost stories, which I adored and definitely added to my interest. I also spent my formative years living in a house which I would love to investigate today, due to some of the occurrences there.

———

My most memorable experience has to be a vigil I shared with Julie Harwood, our group leader, and as an open-minded skeptic it made me question the existence of demonic entities, for want of a better word. We were investigating a suburban three-bedroom semi.

We were aware of a very heavy atmosphere the minute we walked through the door and felt very uneasy. We were alone, in the dark, in the lounge when we both spotted a crouched figure in the corner of the room. It seemed to emanate such menace, and we were very unnerved.

The last straw was a low growling sound coming from the thing in the corner. Our first thought was the sleeping cat on the other sofa, but a quick check showed the animal to be at peace. This did not last, however, and as more growling ensued, the cat stretched up onto its haunches and hissed and spat at whatever was in the corner of that room. It was at this point that we turned the lights on.

———

Don Swain — Paranormal Investigator, Yuma, Arizona

I have been interested in all things paranormal since I was little. I was lucky enough to work with Dave Christensen of Nebraska Paranormal Investigations in my younger years and to learn the dos and don'ts of ghost hunting.

———

One of the most memorable experiences I have had was when I had a team of ghost hunters in from Mesa, Arizona. They were investigating the Lee Hotel here in Yuma. At about 2:00 a.m. they all went to bed (some ghost hunters, huh?).

Anyway, I proceeded to start tearing down my equipment. I was all alone in the lobby and got "chicken skin." When this happens I talk to myself (or the spirits, as the case may be). I always have a tape recorder running and had some excellent interaction with two spirits, one of a male and one of a young girl. They were actually interacting with the things I said. Of course, I didn't know this until I reviewed the tape the next day.

———

(Author's note: I listened to the recordings of EVP, including the one of the spirits he heard interacting with him during the investigation at the Lee Hotel.)

Don: "Here is the first of the EVP I spoke of in the interview. As I said, I was alone in the lobby putting away and loading equipment. I said, 'If you are going to be here you could help me put this stuff away.' Then, you hear in the EVP, a young girl giggles."

EVP: *young girl is definitely heard giggling*

Don: "Then I was picking up a large case to take it to the van. I said, "This case is heavy; you should help carry it!"

EVP: *(little girl's voice)* "Should I move?" *(It was so clear and full of personality. You could hear the hint of mischief in the little girl's giggle, and she seemed to enjoy the fact Don was acknowledging her presence, and was obviously trying to communicate with him.)*

Don: "The next EVP is from the same night. I had finished packing up everything but my recorder. (It always goes out the door with me no matter where I am working.) I said to the spirits, 'I am going upstairs to check the doors. Then I will be out of your house; don't irritate your guests too bad.' I got this EVP …"

EVP: *(young clear voice)* "Going upstairs."

Don: "The next one is from the same night. I came down from upstairs, and the recorder was making a racket (a clicking sound). I said, 'What's wrong with this thing?'"

EVP: *(clear male voice)* "I didn't touch it." *(Then the recorder stopped.)*

Don: "When I got home I checked the recorder. It was an old Sony Pro Style, and the belt had broken. All of these EVP were taken between 2:00 and 3:00 in the morning … these EVP were all collected during a two-day investigation at the Lee Hotel. The first one was recorded right after Linda and I walked in the door."

EVP: (*male voice*) "Ahh, shit!" (*It sounded like he wasn't too pleased with paranormal investigators coming into the hotel to check out his domain. The voice sounded more nervous than annoyed.*)

Don: "The next EVP was taken from a radio DJ's audio tape. He was conducting an interview while I was setting up the Sony Night Shot at the Lee Hotel. He called me a few days later and asked me to listen to this."

EVP: (*very angry male voice*) "Hey, what are you doing? Turn it off!"

Don: "Here is an EVP that came from the GE camcorder during a daytime walk-through, while preparing for an investigation."

EVP: (*very clear female voice*) "Can you hear her?"

Don: "This next EVP came from the Yuma Cemetery, off the Sony Night Shot. I was recording Linda while she was dowsing. My video camera kept shutting off. The battery was full and the system check found no problems. We were in [the] potter's field of the cemetery. When we replayed the tape we found this."

EVP: (*clear child's voice*) "Playing with camcorder."

Don: "The next EVP happened when I stood a wooden headstone back up in the cemetery."

EVP: (*extremely clear and articulate Spanish male voice*) "Muchas gracias."

Don: "Children's voices bother me the most. The 'muchas gracias' EVP is the one that sold me on the belief that spirits have and show emotion. The headstone was in the potter's field of the cemetery, where the illegal immigrants that have died in the desert are buried when they are not claimed."

(*The Conner House was one of the oldest residences in Yuma, Arizona, before it was demolished by the city, and Don and his team conducted an investigation there one night.*)

Don: "The EVP comes through more times than not as a burst type of noise. I truly believe that many ghost hunters miss a lot of EVP because they dismiss the noise as just noise. The original Conner noise is the clearest example of 'raw EVP' I have ever heard. ... Here is the same EVP, except it was loaded into an editing program and slowed down 25 percent. You can hear it more clearly now; it is not such a burst of energy."

EVP: (*clear, female voice*) "Where are you?"

Don: "Under the last EVP another white noise showed on the scope, so when we removed the 'Where are you?' voice we found this under it."

EVP: (*clear, male voice*) "I am here, speak to me."

———

JOHN TALLON — PARANORMAL INVESTIGATOR, CANADIAN HAUNTING AND PARANORMAL SOCIETY

Originally from Sault Ste. Marie, Ontario, I joined the military in 1981 as an aero-engine technician. I was first sent to CFB Petawawa, Ontario, where my job was repairing helicopters. Part of this posting involved two six-month peacekeeping tours in El Gorah, Egypt, on the Sinai Peninsula. In 1989, I moved to Comox, British Columbia, to work on anti-submarine aircraft. The role of this aircraft blossomed into a multi-purpose aircraft involving long-range search and rescue in the Pacific Ocean, fisheries patrols (trying to help eliminate drift-net fishing boats), and pollution control (ships dumping bilges at sea).

In 2000, I returned to CFB Petawawa to work on helicopters. In 2010, I retired from the Regular Force of the Canadian Forces and rejoined as a member of the Primary Reserve. The major change is that I will no longer be posted and will remain in Petawawa as long as I desire.

I joined CHAPS in November 2009 because a friend at the time was holding a training session at her place. I like convenience! I have long been interested in the paranormal as it is something I have been very, very curious about. Part of that deals with a visitation by my grandmother the evening she died. It wasn't a physical presence, but more like seeing her in my mind's eye and knowing that she had passed away. The next morning, I was informed that she had passed away at the time that I had seen her.

———

We were investigating a home near Barrie, Ontario. I was kneeling in a doorway videotaping three women in a small room. I was wearing a flashlight on my back belt loop just in case we needed light. I remember this sensation as being similar to a fish testing the bait of a fisherman. I felt two quick, light tugs on the flashlight I had clipped to my belt loop. I thought that I had backed into the stairwell, but on looking behind me the stairwell was two feet away. I was shocked, amazed, and surprised for a moment. (I jumped to my feet yelling, "Who grabbed my flashlight!" and spun like a top for a few seconds.)

A moment later, after I had regained my composure, a girl in the next room who was asking questions spun and yelled, "Who grabbed my T-shirt?" Nobody was anywhere near either of us, but we both had our first physical encounters at the same place on the same night. It was pretty cool, in hindsight!

5

SPIRITS, GHOSTS, AND HAUNTINGS

I've received many emails that begin with the words: "There is *something* in my house too ..."

A lot of people are reluctant, or perhaps unable, to define the encounters they have had. If there is no other natural explanation, it's possible there is a supernatural cause. If that is so, is it an earthbound ghost, the spirit of a loved one, or residual energy causing the activity?

Knowing more about the ghost/spirit is important if dealing with a haunting, to understand why it might be occurring and what can be learned from it.

Everyone, at one time or another, has jumped out from around a corner or behind a door, wanting to startle a friend or younger sibling, just for the humour in seeing their reaction. It seems some spirits might maintain that same sense of harmless mischief, and want nothing more than a humorous, startled response when they have an opportunity to instigate it.

But quite often an encounter with a spirit has nothing to do with mischief or humour, and everything to do with still needing to have a connection with others, which we all do. And often these attempts at connecting are made when help is needed, either by the spirits or for those haunted by them.

———

ADVICE AND INSIGHT

HEATHER ANDERSON — PARANORMAL INVESTIGATOR

I am of the opinion that a ghost would have a personality much as they would have when they were alive. I think that since we do not fully understand hauntings, people can feel threatened by their experiences even though there is no intent to harm. We have only had one report where someone felt that a ghost/spirit hurt them, but this may have been caused by natural occurrences or actions caused by the witness, and not at all a malevolent spirit. If we are correct in that spirits/ghosts are ethereal impressions of a human, it stands to reason that their personality follows them in the afterlife.

Our own reports show that hauntings generally occur at a location, although there have been cases where a haunting seems to follow a person. I am unsure whether this is due to the fact that a person seems to be more open to these kinds of occurrences or whether an actual following occurs.

A ghost would act as one would expect a living human to, and if you were to ask one politely to leave, a co-operative ghost may do so. Some people rely upon their spiritual beliefs and perform rituals to encourage the spirit to leave. When I am confronted by a frightened witness who wishes their home to remain "ghost-free," I usually tell them to "reclaim" their home, to ask politely out loud for whatever it is to leave. This has been our standard recourse in this situation. Whether it is simply the witness feeling empowered in reclaiming their home or whether there was a spirit that has actually left, we have found this quite effective, and our witnesses tell us that they have felt much more comfortable in their homes after they have accomplished this.

In the past, it seems that belief in ghosts/spirits/paranormal was indeed there; however, today we are more willing to talk about it as more than just parlour tricks and ghost stories around campfires. We cannot dispute that people *are* having these experiences; however, what these experiences actually are, we still do not know. People today are more interested in the why and how of hauntings, what causes them and how they exist. They want to measure the activity, find some tangible evidence of their existence. To date, I do not think this has been achieved, although I am quite interested in EVP, and we hope to perform more studies on this.

———

RONA ANDERSON — PARANORMAL INVESTIGATOR AND PSYCHIC MEDIUM

Spirits and ghosts are just different names for the souls of people and animals who have died and left their bodies. Although people tend to call souls that haunt a place "ghosts." It's the word *ghosts* that is used in a scary way, and *spirits* just doesn't have the same scary connotations.

The majority of spirits are benevolent. The earthbound spirits sometimes have problems like needing to scare people for their energy or continuing to do the same negative things they did in life, like molesting people, feeding off of people's addictions because they are addicts, inflicting their bad habits or negative emotions on people. I do *not* believe in demons. They are more of a belief by certain religions, and a Hollywood effect in TV shows and movies to scare people.

Ghosts are attracted to energies, whether it is in the land or a building or a person. Some of them have died in a particular house or piece of land; however, that is an exception, not a rule. We have gone to brand-new condo buildings and century-old houses, and they sometimes contain a spirit or spirits that are there for their own personal reasons: they used to live in a house like this; the young girl/boy reminds them of their child; they love the family's interaction with each other;

they are sexually attracted to a certain person; they like the dog/cat; they have the same hobby or interest as the homeowner; the person living in the house has the same addiction the spirit has to alcohol or drugs; or someone in the house has a "victim energy" (they were abused in some way in their lives) and the spirit is a rapist, child molester, wife beater, etc., who is tormenting them in some way.

Some people can get spirit attachments, and it can be for various reasons. Sometimes the living were in a former life with that particular spirit. As mentioned before, the person might have a victim energy and a negative spirit has attached themselves. Addicts often get spirit attachments who are feeding off their addictions and are constantly around them. If you're an addict, the only way to stop spirits attaching themselves to you is to get clean. If you do have a spirit attachment, you have to take a long look at yourself and assess what they could be attracted to.

I know of many ways people have tried to get spirits to leave a location. Sometimes when you are firm, unafraid, and tell them they are not welcome and would they please leave, some have. The majority of times people will call in a priest, smudge their house with sage and herbs, perform a religious ceremony. The spirit will leave temporarily, but can eventually come back because they were not sent into the light. They left because they were irritated by the goings-on, and the religious stuff has no effect on them. Negative spirits are the worst to try and get to leave. You need to have a spirit removal or spirit rescue person come in and actually be able to communicate with the spirit and send them over, or into the light, which people can think of as heaven, another plane or dimension. Then they are permanently gone from that person's house and not allowed to come back. This doesn't happen with loved ones such as relatives and friends. Usually they have crossed over and are allowed to come back to visit.

The majority of people I have talked to believe in ghosts and have either experienced something or know someone who has. Unfortunately, the TV shows and movies portray ghosts and hauntings as horror and demonic attacks.

The skeptics who cite science as their measuring stick say, "If I can't touch it, taste it, or see it, it doesn't exist. Prove it." Yet many of them have religious beliefs in some deity they can't see or hear. They believe in scientific things that we can't see, but since a scientist says it's so, it is so. I have found that actually, they are afraid of the paranormal and usually of death itself. I have asked some skeptics to come into a darkened room or particular place with me that is supposed to be haunted and sit for ten to fifteen minutes, and every one of them declined saying either they don't want to sit in the dark or it's just wasting their time. They appear nervous and uneasy.

There is truly nothing to be afraid of once you begin to understand spirits and the afterlife. They only want to be acknowledged and remembered.

——————

JILL BRUENER — PSYCHIC, MEDIUM, CLAIRVOYANT, AND SPIRITUAL ADVISOR

There is a difference between a spirit and a ghost. What we term a ghost is an earthbound soul. This means that this particular soul did not cross over and go into the light. The most common reasons for not crossing over are fear of going to hell, a traumatic death, untimely death, a need to stay and watch over the family, or not knowing they are dead. Some feel they have unfinished business, and others feel they need some type of closure.

Our society, over the centuries, has made such a farce out of ghosts. I can remember watching *Casper the Friendly Ghost* cartoons as a child and wondering why those idiots were afraid and would run away screaming. We have to remember that ghosts are just discarnate souls. They are people, just like you and me. They are somebody's mother, father, brother, sister, daughter, or son. They are just lost souls. We should have compassion for them and for their situation. Can you imagine what it must feel like to be trapped in limbo? There is such a fine line between the spirit world and ours.

Ghosts have different ways of haunting (which is derived from the French word meaning "to frequent"). They are just going about their business. Most of the time they are not even aware of us. Remember, we are usually living in their house; they were there first. Some ghosts just go about their daily chores. Others replay the same scenario over and over again, such as their murder or their death scene. Others will rap, knock, move things, or take things and then return them. Other times people will hear footsteps, feel a chill, smell odours, or feel like someone is watching them or standing by them. When this happens they are only trying to get our attention. We, as living human beings, have an aura. That is the electromagnetic field that surrounds our body.

Ghosts will sometimes see us only as energy patterns. If you were trapped in the dark and trying to get out you would be drawn to any type of light source, thinking this would be the way out and into the light. Some people's auras are only as strong as a birthday candle, others like a flashlight, and still others like a beacon of light. Ghosts are only looking for help most of the time. They are trying to get our attention to say, "Please help me." They do not really do things to intentionally scare us.

As a psychic/medium, I feel it is my job to do soul rescue for these poor unfortunate souls. I get numerous calls where people believe they have a ghost in their house. With my gift, I can walk through a house and tell if there is a ghost there and who it is. I can tell if there is more than one, and communicate with them so I can help them cross over into the light. I have compassion for them and want to help them go to God.

Spirit is totally different from a ghost. A spirit is a soul that has crossed over and gone into the light. My father is a good example of being in spirit. I now live in the house my parents bought when I was one, which means I have been associated with this house since then. My father crossed over in 1994, and I bought the house. My father is very active in this house, and I feel him around all the time. He loves to open the front door and also to sit in his favourite chair. He is also fond of opening my bedroom door at night and coming in and sitting on the side of my bed. He always shows up when I am upset or depressed. His presence is very comforting, and he just pops in and out when he wants to. His soul is not trapped here, and he's not here all the time. He is what is referred to as a reverent spirit, which means he has the ability to travel back and forth between the other side and Earth. Spirit has the ability to travel back and forth from the other side to the earth plane whenever they choose. They are not earthbound like a ghost.

Our master guides/teachers are also in spirit. These are souls that have lived before and have now chosen to be our guides from the other side. The difference is that spirits are highly evolved and they have the understanding of the other side. They have the ability to visit back and forth. Ghosts, on the other hand, are trapped souls who have not crossed over into the Light. They may still hang on to old negative human emotions such as fear, jealousy, anger, hatred, and resentment. Spirit is enlightened. They have shed all of the negative human emotions. They only feel love, joy, peace of mind, and God's love. They have now become one with the Christ-conscious energy.

It has been my experience that 99.9 percent of the ghosts and spirits that I have encountered have been benevolent. Maybe because I look at them as human souls. I have love and compassion for them like I would any human being. Ghosts don't want to be in their situation, they just are. They are only looking for help.

———

STEPHEN BOSTON — PARANORMAL INVESTIGATOR AND TECHNICAL TRAINER

Personally, I think spirits and ghosts are very much one and the same. However, if I were pushed to give a specific answer, I would say that a ghost could be more of a residual energy left in an area or a building, whereas I would class a spirit as a more interactive entity more common in an intelligent haunting where physical interaction takes place.

The majority of living people are of a good nature; however, there are a small minority who are not. I think we can follow this theory into the spirit world.

I think that the majority of location-specific hauntings are due to residual energy and not necessarily intelligent haunting. When an intelligent haunting is set to a specific location, it could be due to a number of factors. A family member or loved one could still reside in the building, drawing them back. A specific event or even the death of the person could also be a draw to the location, or it could simply be a place that held fond memories for them.

I think the field of paranormal research and investigation has been thrust into the public eye over the last few years with shows such as *Ghost Hunters*, *Ghost Adventures*, and *Most Haunted*. I think most people rightly err on the side of skepticism when it comes to TV shows presenting evidence, and there are certainly some shows and teams that are more reputable than others, mentioning no names. Generally, I think most people are open to the idea that these things go on; however, few are willing to actually spend hours sitting around old houses in the dark actually looking for it.

———

WENDY CALLAWAY — PARANORMAL INVESTIGATOR

I don't believe that a ghost/spirit can cause you serious harm; however, I also don't believe that they are all benevolent, as I have certainly had experiences to the contrary.

I personally like calling out, letting spirits know that we are not there to harm them in any way, and asking very specific questions. Over the last couple of years I have heard some amazing responses on voice recorders and video footage in reply to questions asked, when footage has been reviewed.

There could be any number of reasons why a ghost/spirit will haunt a specific location. It could be somewhere where they have unfinished business, where somebody close to them lives, where they died, where a significant event in their lives occurred. In my opinion, trying to identify why the spirit is tied to that location would be key.

In my experience, the majority of people's initial reaction is that I'm a little bit crazy for doing paranormal investigations. However, I have been surprised how many people have then approached me and asked for advice on something that's happened, or told me of an experience that they have had. Many are very interested in findings from investigations that I attend.

———

LISA CARTER — PARANORMAL INVESTIGATOR

People hold on to their loved ones and often hope they are there watching them and comforting them. Or the living person may feel threatened or scared, but the spirit is only there to find comfort in their company.

Some places have energies from years of heartache or emotional subject matter that pertains to that area. Hospitals and graveyards are least likely to be haunted, whereas city parks, jails, and private residences are hot spots.

I believe that there is a mixed view on the subject of ghosts and hauntings. Some believe in their existence, some completely reject the thought due to either personal disbelief or religious views. It is a touchy subject for some, and I believe that if paranormal phenomena were to happen to the non-believers it may change their views. It is one of those subjects that you are either for or against.

―――――

BARRI GHAI — PARANORMAL INVESTIGATOR

In my opinion, there is no difference between a ghost and a spirit. There are various forms of spirit, but the word *ghost* is simply a name for phenomena which have been categorized by popular culture and myth for centuries.

There are different forms of a spirit, though. These are commonly categorized into four main areas: intelligent hauntings, residual haunt-ings, poltergeist phenomena, and demonic entity.

Through my many personal experiences, I would tend to believe that most ghosts or spirits are benevolent. I have only ever encountered one truly evil entity, and this was definitely demonic in origin. In 99 percent of all cases I have personally investigated, there have only ever been a few reports where individuals have been physically attacked or injured by an unseen force.

It is, however, becoming increasingly common for people to report experiences of negative feeling, oppression, or possible threats in one form or another. I feel that if spirits are the souls of those once living, it should be conceivable that many of them would be just as obnoxious or bad-tempered in death as they may have been in life!

Ghosts can haunt specific locations because they may have been tied to that place physically or emotionally during their life. A typical haunting is based upon this very fact and would be dictated by a spirit remaining bound to a certain location. I think this is so common because by nature human beings are passionate creatures. We yearn for comfort and security and are proud to make homes or feel a sense of achievement in our lives. In death the spirit remains bound to these places that held such meaning and comfort to them.

In many cases of reported hauntings, it has been established that the cause of the disturbances is often the spirits of those people who lived or worked at the location affected. The reported paranormal activity may become more frequent or simply begin after building work or even simple decoration has taken place, which it appears may have upset the former tenant, owner, or worker.

In other cases, when people die quickly or violently their spirits are often left in a limbo state, which most likely remains bound to the specific location of their death. Often they do not want to leave the world they were so happy in, or they just cannot accept that they are dead.

A person can be haunted rather than a place. Paranormal experts refer to this as a spirit attachment, possession, or simply a personal haunting. This type of affliction can be caused by dabbling with the occult or playing with Ouija boards, for example. It can also be caused by an unrealized psychic gift, [or one] that the person has not been able to learn to use properly. Vulnerable individuals are often weak in mind and body, and normally have been through a traumatic event that has acted as a catalyst.

In some cases, it is just poor unfortunate people who have literally attracted the spirit to them by exuding high levels of life force. Basically, they shine bright into the spirit world, and their force is so strong it acts like a flame to a moth.

Another cause for this is a "curse." In many cultures around the world, especially Asian traditions, a curse can be bestowed by offering food or drink and often gives the recipient a spirit attachment that literally steals their life and ultimately causes physical signs of depression, sickness, and, on occasion, death.

There is no fixed science to remove spirits from a location. Traditional methods include burning white sage, candles, and incense sticks. Other people believe that prayer and the power of love can remove an unwanted spirit from a location. In my experience and opinion, the power of self-belief and the absence of fear work. Fear is a very powerful emotion and one that spirits use to absorb as energy to fuel their manifestations or activity. To remove their power, one should feel confident to take control and take back ownership of the location, whether it is a home or workplace.

My society does use the skills of a spiritual medium in exceptional circumstances. She is skilled at helping unwanted or troubled spirits to leave their earthly confinements and cross over to the spirit realm by means of blessings, sound, and the burning of sage. Her ability to see and speak to spirits helps act as a mediatory link, and therefore this seems to be the most effective way to get rid of spirits from a location.

The subject of ghosts and hauntings remains fascinating to most people. The issue is still treated as taboo in many cultures across the developed world, and does get dismissed as rubbish or mere fantasy by many. However, this view is helped and hindered by the rise of films and television programs like *Medium*, *Supernatural*, *The Exorcism of Emily Rose*, *The Rite*, and *Insidious*.

The fascination with the unknown remains extremely high, and the curiosity in us all keeps this subject at the front of our modern world and threads of popular culture. People are scared of what they do not know. People fear the unknown, and if believing is seeing and seeing is believing, then the notion that ghosts exist will keep society intrigued indefinitely.

———

DAVE GIBB — PARANORMAL INVESTIGATOR

I use the term *spirit*; *ghost* is more something we use for lack of a better term.

I believe once we pass we move on to another form of living. Sort of like the Borg from *Star Trek*, to make it simple: a collective that assists us poor saps on the living planet. Sometimes we have learned enough in life and we move on to make that collective, sometimes we move on to another life, and sometimes we are in between overlooking or learning some more. This is my personal belief, and why I continue to search for these answers in as scientific a way as I can.

I have rarely come across a spirit that is not benevolent. If they are not, it is my belief they are frustrated or confused.

I believe it to be possible that spirit can be attached to a person rather than a location. It makes sense: if you were in love with someone, would you not want to stay with them?

I still believe society sees the subject of ghosts and hauntings with disbelief and shock, yet the interest is very high. So all in all it is becoming more positive, at least with recent media attention and shows. Mind you, some of those shows do tend to portray us in a silly light, as do many of the teams out there that are sensational with their approach and lack of maturity.

I'm proud to be a representative of The Atlantic Paranormal Society. It ensures that what we put out is quality product. CHAPS has been held to a bar of excellence that I believe we leap over every time we investigate.

———

JULIE HARWOOD — PARANORMAL INVESTIGATOR

In the paranormal community, I believe a ghost is considered like an old tape recording replaying time and time again and getting fainter each time. These apparitions are not thought to be intelligent and able to interact in anyway. A spirit, I believe, is considered to be an intelligent haunting, able to interact and/or affect their surroundings. They have returned to a place/building/person/object due to either unfinished business or a strong attachment (emotional, physical, etc.).

I strongly believe that if ghosts or spirits do exist in our time, then there will be a mix of personalities. If a person was benevolent in life then I think they will take this on with them; similarly if they are malevolent. However, another strong belief I have is that if they do exist, no spirit can hurt us as we have the strongest thing, and that is a life force.

I believe ghosts are said to haunt specific locations because of the time they spent there. The Stone Tape theory means that if someone did something repeatedly over years (i.e., a maid carrying a pile of towels along a corridor to her master's room), they leave an energy or imprint on the building, like a recording, so even when they are not there anymore it keeps replaying over and over. In regards to why spirits are said to haunt locations, I believe this is because of either unfinished business or an attachment which in some way means they feel they have to or want to return.

———

NICKI HIMMELMAN — PARANORMAL INVESTIGATOR

In my opinion, a ghost is someone who has not yet crossed over and is stuck here on earth; a spirit, however, is one who comes and goes between realms in visitation.

My belief is that spirits/ghosts are human energy. I would say that personalities stay with us after we pass on. I believe that if you were a jerk on earth, odds are you will be a jerk in spirit.

Ghosts that haunt specific locations have an emotional attachment to the location.

I believe the spirits of our loved ones surround us at times. We can pick up on their presence, especially if they are trying to send us a message. Sometime a visitation allows us to see, hear, or smell their presence, and it can be mistaken for a haunting. I also think that spirits are attracted to certain people who are sensitive, especially if they need help.

I believe that the majority of people are open-minded about this, and with the number of paranormal shows on TV, I think our field is becoming more popular and respected by society. Of course, you will always have the skeptics, but in general, I believe, even though we live in such a fast-paced, technological world, the paranormal still surrounds us and people still have experiences. We are all still looking for answers.

———

SCOTT HOBBS — PARANORMAL INVESTIGATOR

There really is no hard evidence as to what ghosts or spirits really are. Folklore would say it is the spirit of someone or something formerly living, but there are also many other theories as to what could cause these paranormal activities that happen.

Our team, like many others, tries to focus on the collection of data and facts rather than trying to guess at what ghosts really are. Hopefully, science can someday answer that question for us.

We've encountered seemingly paranormal entities (for lack of a better term) on a fair number of occasions. We've never felt that our team or the families we were helping were in any danger from these entities. Most of the direct responses we've gotten through audio, video, or by other means seem to indicate looking for help or answers, or perhaps just trying to communicate. We've even come across a home where the spirit seemed intent on playing pranks on us ... making noises one room over from where our team members were. It felt like we were part of a game.

If spirits were in fact people, I would venture that they would have the same motivations as the living: some have evil or negative intent ... the vast majority do not.

Is it possible that a person, rather than an actual place, can be haunted? I didn't used to believe it, but then I met Joe [not his real name]. He and his girlfriend asked us to investigate their home because Joe had been experiencing things at every house he'd lived in. In all honesty, while we were investigating the home we found it almost comedic that he would get spooked by every sound, movement, cool spot, and so on. A couple members of our team even suggested to me in private that he might have some form of mental illness. It wasn't until we went over our audio recordings that we heard direct answers to some of our questions related to Joe, including why it was tormenting him. It seemed like it wasn't comfortable with someone or something in the home. It also mentioned Joe by name. Pretty interesting stuff.

This subject is certainly less taboo than it was twenty years ago. I suppose it is the upside of the over-the-top television programs out there about the paranormal. I've read that as many as 50 percent of people in North America now believe in ghosts.

The downside, of course, is that because of these shows, many who watch them now believe they are experts in the field. It has caused a lot of trouble for legitimate investigation teams, since now there are a number of people running around with EMF detectors thinking they know all there is to know. (I won't get into the fact that EMF and the paranormal is a totally unproven theory.)

All that said, it is inviting to know that more people tend to be open to the idea of the paranormal. When we started our team, there were always those underlying fears that everyone would think we were off our rockers. The number of calls and emails we get has proven to us we were probably worrying for nothing.

MARIE HOLDER — PARANORMAL INVESTIGATOR

I would say the majority (but not all) of ghosts, spirits, or energies I have experienced have been benevolent, but of course, as in life, there are those that are malevolent.

I believe there are different theories about why ghosts haunt specific locations. They could have died there, and the manner of their passing could have been such that they felt the need to return to the place of their death, or they lived there at one time and it brought back pleasant memories for them so they chose to return. There is the Stone Tape theory, which suggests that within the brickwork of each building is the essence of the people who lived there and that the hauntings that occur are playbacks of those lifetimes.

I've had a lot of mixed reactions when talking about the paranormal as a whole. Some people are really interested in what I do and always ask the same sort of questions: "Have you seen anything?" or "Don't you get scared?" There are, however, people that think it's a load of rubbish! I don't think the numbers of people that are open to the idea are getting any less, as we are always coming up with ways of trying to prove their existence, with new technologies being thought of all the time.

AMANDA HORLEY — PARANORMAL INVESTIGATOR

To me, a ghost is a physical apparition. A manifestation of energy. It might be sentient and aware of our presence and willing to interact with us, or it might be residual energy and not be aware of our presence. A spirit is unseen (more felt or sensed) energy. I tend to think of a spirit as an energy that will interact with us in some way, rather than residual energy.

As with living people, they are probably mostly benevolent, but I do believe that, as in life, there are energies that are bad. I don't believe that the majority of them are capable of physically harming us, but they can instill feelings of fear or terror in a person, if that person is susceptible to picking up on energies. If we do not accept that they can do us harm, I think that will be the case. Those that are aware of our presence are generally fine with us, sometimes co-operative and sometimes curious, but seldom give the impression of wanting to harm us.

Why do ghosts haunt specific locations? A mix of reasons. If you are talking about residual energy, then it will probably be somewhere they spent a lot of time, such as a workplace or home. If it is interactive energy, then it could be somewhere that they were very happy, or similarly could be somewhere where they had something very traumatic happen to them or even where they died. They do not necessarily appear to be the age they were at death. For example, I know a female spirit who was sixty when she died, but always comes across as being in her late teens.

I do not believe that a person can be haunted. Objects can be haunted in the same way as places, and a person could be carrying an object with a strong energy attached to it which could linger around the person. An energy may also choose to be close to a living person and may travel around with them, but they are still two separate entities. Actually, I think I have just contradicted myself here, as if a person has an energy travelling around with them, I suppose some people would refer to that person as being haunted. Personally, though, I would only describe a person as haunted if they had been taken over by a spirit and their own personality had been subdued, and that to me is a medical condition, not a haunting.

I have never made a human spirit leave a location and do not believe I have the right to do so or the capability. If a current owner/occupier is adamant that they want the spirit to go, then you can ask it to consider moving on, and maybe put forward arguments toward this end. Also, especially in the case of a child or a spirit that is distressed, it can help to discuss the possibility of moving to the light and passing on and how they will feel better for this. However, this will, of course, only work on spirits that interact with us rather than residual energies, and the final decision has to be theirs. I do not believe that spirits or residual energies can be forced to leave a location.

Whilst I will, on very rare occasions (as the circumstances dictate) point out to a spirit that moving on is a possibility and it might want to consider this as a course of action, I broke my own rules when my cat died. She had been with me for almost twenty years, and I didn't handle her death well. After two evenings of listening to her spirit moving around the house, footsteps on the stairs and in the bathroom, her name tag banging against her food bowl, I did ask her to go. I just couldn't cope with her still being so obviously present. I told her about the light and explained that she was dead and could no longer stay with me. I asked her go to the light and tried to explain to her that it would be better for her as well as me if she moved on. That was the last night that I was aware of her as a spirit presence in the house. However, even in this case, I prefer to think that she chose to go and so reduce my pain. By the way, there is still some residual energy of her around, particularly around the bottom of the stairs, but this is no longer disturbing.

The majority of people who offer an opinion will laugh and belittle you being a paranormal investigator, but it is surprising how many say very little, and when pressed have had unexplained experiences themselves. Generally it seems to be accepted behaviour to treat ghosts, hauntings, and paranormal investigators as something to make fun of and something that shouldn't be taken seriously. This has been made worse by TV programs such as *Most Haunted*, which people seem to take as fact and truth or alternatively to treat as a laughingstock; in fact, all they are is a piece of entertainment. Less obvious, but equally as strong, are the religious objections. I know my sister feels that what I do is wrong. The religious objectors tend to be less vocal that the belittlers. I do, however, feel that a lot of people will react as they think society expects them to. As I said, I know many people who don't generally offer an opinion on the subject will, when drawn into a conversation about it, relate experiences they can't explain and will admit that they have wondered if maybe ghosts and hauntings are a possibility after all.

JAMIE JACKSON — PARANORMAL INVESTIGATOR

I tend to use the words *ghost* and *spirit* synonymously; however, I know technically the term *spirit* relates to the soul or essence of a living thing. Most spirits can move about and go where they please. A ghost or apparition is more connected with a haunting and generally stays connected with one place. An analogy would be a spirit is like an albatross, able to fly wherever it pleases; whereas a ghost is more like an ostrich, capable of movement, but without the freedom of flight. Both are birds, but they both have different lives.

One of the most common reasons ghosts haunts a specific location is that there is a violent or sudden death, and the spirits either don't realize they are dead or don't believe they are allowed to cross over. Take Gettysburg, for instance. The men there died very violently, and they took other lives as well. I believe most of the ghosts there think that because they took other lives they are unworthy to cross over. Also, many probably think they are still alive reliving the battle.

I think that most people are skeptics, but they are still curious and wonder, "What if?" I have noticed a huge surge in ghost hunting and the paranormal, and I think that there will be another spiritual revolution in the next few years. Most people I encounter, such as the people who develop my film and the people whom I buy electronic equipment from, are always curious about what I do and want to tag along on a hunt.

KIMBERLEY LAPIERRE — PARANORMAL INVESTIGATOR

A ghost is someone who passes away but does not cross over to the other side, while a spirit is someone who has crossed over and occasionally comes back to check on loved ones from time to time. Ghosts are trapped here, unless someone helps them to cross over, while spirits are free to come and go as they please. Most people, and even some paranormal groups, use the two terms interchangeably, but I firmly believe they are completely different in nature.

There are many reasons deceased persons may choose not to cross over. It may be because they have done some horrible things in their lives and they fear they will be judged for their actions. Sometimes it's because they die suddenly in a tragic way and do not realize that they are dead. Some choose to stay to ensure their loved ones are okay. Whatever the reason, if they weren't very nice when they were alive, they remain that way until they cross over.

Ghosts retain the same personalities they had in life and will act accordingly. If someone was a jerk and a bully in life, you can bet they will be the same way as a ghost. This is why we sometimes come across very hostile ghosts who are angered by our presence, while there are others who seek us out because they know that our intentions are good and we are there to help them. Just like you can't reason with some people, sometimes you can't reason with some ghosts.

Ghosts can haunt a location for any number of reasons. The most common reason is because it is the area where they lost their life suddenly, and they are still wandering around unaware that they are dead. Time has no meaning to them, so they do not realize that many years or decades may have passed. Ghosts are also known to haunt places that hold a special meaning to them. It could be the family home, a favourite park, a cottage they spent summers at as a child. Whatever the reason or location, they will remain trapped there until they can find a way to cross over.

Ghosts can become attached to a person and focus all of their energy on getting their attention. A person may choose to stay behind after they die because they feel a sense of obligation to watch out for a loved one who is still living. That, in a sense, is a haunting. In other cases, like the story depicted in the movie *The Sixth Sense*, ghosts may not be aware that they are dead, so they remain near the ones they love, doing the things they would normally do. The living mistakenly believe this to be a haunting, when in fact the ghost is totally unaware of their demise. Whether the intentions or the reasons for the attachment are good or bad, people can be haunted by a ghost.

Spirits may come and go as they please, as they've crossed over to the other side. If you do not wish to have them pop in and visit you, you could ask them not to, and they will happily abide by your wishes as they want only what is best for you and come from a place of light and love.

However, if you'd like to get a ghost to leave a location it takes a little more work. We try to appease any fears they may have that have kept them from crossing over. We explain that there is no judgment and that all their loved ones are waiting for them on the other side to welcome them home. We also let them know that they will be able to return to check on their loved ones, so they needn't fear leaving them behind. Once we've helped them to understand that there is a better place for them to be, most happily cross over and join their loved ones on the other side. However, if someone chooses to stay it is their free will, and we cannot make them go.

We smudge locations where ghosts are known to remain in an effort to bring them the peace they need to move on. Smudging is the burning of herbs or incense for cleansing, purification, protection of physical and spiritual bodies, banishment of negative energies, and creation of sacred space. Shamanic smudging releases the energy and fragrance of the herbs and botanicals so they can heal, cleanse, and purify.

I believe that there are more people in this world who have had experiences than those who have not. With the popularity of shows dealing with paranormal research and those that recount personal experiences of both everyday people and celebrities, more people have reached a level where they are quite comfortable discussing their experiences, and it's no longer considered taboo.

As more and more everyday people come forward to share their stories, the stigmatism of being "crazy" that was once associated with paranormal experiences has pretty much fallen to the wayside. However, as in any field, there will always be skeptics, no matter how much evidence is gathered and presented by paranormal researchers. Some people just won't believe until they can see it, hear it, or touch it for themselves."

———

IAN MURPHY — PARANORMAL INVESTIGATOR

In common mythology, people do not believe there is a difference between a spirit and a ghost. Just interchangeable terms, used usually in different parts of the world and across cultures. As a scientific research team, we are looking to prove or disprove the existence of paranormal events. At this time, we have no proof to either end.

In classic theories of spirits/ghosts, a unifying theory is that it is the conscience of a person, and as such people have the ability to be benevolent or not, so there is the variation of personality in spirits.

The theory is that ghosts will stay in a location that they are familiar with, insomuch as people find solace in the areas they are used to.

It is eminently more likely for a person to be haunted than a location. This is because their experiences may be the result of a chemical interaction on the neurological level, evidence of past trauma, or other [the result of] psychological issues that may be affecting them. While not a classic haunting, they do feel real to the person experiencing them.

The first step is to address any natural/psychological issues that may be the root cause of the haunting. Only after eliminating the natural can we even begin to delve into the supernatural.

———

DR. DAVE OESTER — PARANORMAL INVESTIGATOR

Ghosts and spirits are the same. It is the essence of who they were in life that we would call the soul. The soul is just another name for spirit or for ghost. Some groups try to separate the meaning for each, but the bottom line is that the name that is applied is based on the individual's background and need to find closure regarding death. If our loved ones return to watch over us, are they ghosts or spirits? Generally most people would respond, "If it is my deceased family member than it is a spirit, but if it is someone I don't know than it is a ghost."

Most spirits are as they were in life. If they were happy, then they will be spirits who are happy and content. However, if they were angry in life, that anger continues with them beyond the grave. Often these angry ghosts are confused and thought to be demons or evil spirits. Spirits retain their intelligence, their emotions, and their personality after death.

Generally, unfinished business or unresolved issues anchor a spirit to this dimension. Often, negative emotional issues that were not resolved in life must still be dealt with in death. Some spirits are comfortable here and have no desire to move on. There are probably as many reasons why a spirit would remain as there are people. Ghosts are people without physical bodies.

No exorcism will be effective if the spirit or spirits do not want to depart. God does not save the life of a child, nor does He move spirits along simply because we want Him to do it. Spirits have reasons for remaining here, and they will not depart until those issues or reasons are completed. Spirits are not under the same understanding of religion as the living. Religious names, rituals, icons, blessed water, sage sticks, or cleansing rituals have no effect, unless the spirit is ready to move on. In many cases if a cleansing is attempted, the spirit may respond in revenge. Imagine someone telling you to get out of your home. You would respond in a negative manner. The only way is to simply ask them to move to some other dwelling and explain to them why you are asking.

Society's reaction is based in large part on how Hollywood portrays the spirits of the dead. Society tends to view ghosts in whatever light that current movies portray them. We have had over 3 million visitors to our website, where we teach that ghosts are just people without physical bodies. They have feelings and can become angry or happy because there is life after death, and in that new life they are very much alive and well. We have been teaching people how to document the existence of life after death since 1996. We help people understand that they should not fear death, as religion and society suggest. Life does go beyond the grave and love does survive the grave.

SARAH PETTET — PARANORMAL INVESTIGATOR

Personally, I think there is a difference between a spirit and a ghost. To my mind a ghost is more residual, something that is appearing in the same place again and again. A spirit to me would be a more intelligent haunting, something that is able to interact with surroundings or people.

I think they have as much benevolence as we all do. We, as human beings, make decisions or take actions that can be good or bad; I don't think that is going to change much when we are dead. Having said that, I have, in my time as an investigator, only encountered one or two spirits/ghosts that have made me feel uneasy.

I think it is possible that a person, rather than an actual place, can be haunted — particularly by an intelligent haunting. It's almost as if the person has been latched on to. One of my siblings died a few years ago, and a friend who is a spiritual medium often sees my sibling either at my house or at my other sister's house, and my sister has moved houses since my sibling died.

How society reacts toward ghosts and haunting, I think, varies depending on the person. There are complete skeptics, complete believers, and those that are in between (as we have in our investigation team); how boring would it be if everyone agreed! I think the majority of people are a bit unsure, and some will make a bit of a joke about it, but most are curious and want to know one way or another. I have found when I tell people what I do in my spare time they are very interested and ask questions regardless of what they believe.

———

LYNSEY ROBSON — PARANORMAL INVESTIGATOR

There are varying opinions on the differences between a ghost and a spirit. The common consensus is that a ghost is simply a deceased person who has yet to pass to another realm, whereas a spirit is a supernatural being. The words are used so interchangeably that I believe that there is very little difference between the two in the modern world.

My own beliefs on this subject are quite strong. I wholeheartedly believe that spirits/ghosts aren't ill-willed. I believe they are just like the living in that there are good and bad eggs. I believe the majority of activity that is interpreted as "evil" or "malevolent" is in fact just a plea for attention or a cry out in confusion.

My thoughts on why ghosts haunt specific locations is just that, my own thoughts. I believe that the reason they choose specific locations is because there is some tie to that location in life. It may be that they lived there for a time, a person they cared about lived there, they worked there, or perhaps the location reminded them of something.

I believe it very possible that a person can be the tie that a spirit is attached to, rather than a place. I think that the majority of the time, a spirit becomes attached to a location, as locations generally are around longer than a person. People move constantly, so that could be very difficult to follow, but I do believe it happens.

If you want someone to leave, you ask them to leave. I believe it's similar when dealing with spirits. It's always important to remember that these spirits may be there for a reason, they may be trying to get your help, so if you're uncomfortable with their presence, I think the best thing you can do is seek help to cross the spirits over.

I still think there's a huge stigma surrounding anything paranormal. It seems society as a whole has regressed in this feeling. If it can't been seen, touched, or proven 100 percent, it can't be true. Those who believe are those who have experienced something, or know someone to have experienced something.

MARIA STREET — PARANORMAL INVESTIGATOR

I think the literal translation is that a ghost is a vision, a residual haunting, and cannot be communicated with in any way. I believe it is a replay of the past and in some cases may be a Stone Tape recording. A spirit is more tangible and can be communicated with.

The more you believe in their existence, the more you believe in their good/evil intentions. If I were to put it any way, I would suggest they are the same as they were in life. Why would a personality change with death?

I think society's reaction to this subject is improving, and this is largely to do with the media and its plethora of paranormal programming. Some programs, which are for entertainment purposes only, are vilified, but on the whole most are respected for their unbiased and factual accounts of the investigations they conduct, and this has sparked interest in a lot of viewers, particularly those who tune in for the thrill factor and find themselves totally engrossed and fascinated by the whole subject.

―――――

DON SWAIN — PARANORMAL INVESTIGATOR

My belief is that the most common haunting that occurs is not a haunting at all. It is called a residual haunting. This is when something has either happened over and over at the same time in the same place, or something has taken place that is so horrific that the energy of the act is imprinted on the environment like a recording, and this causes the act to be replayed over and over.

There are three reasons for most true hauntings.

First, the person has unfinished business. Surprisingly enough, sometimes by grieving too much for a lost loved one we are the ones who hold them to this realm by grieving for them in such a way that they feel they have unfinished business because they cannot cross over until the person grieving is ready to accept the loss.

The second reason is that the person does not know they have died. Most times they were killed in a tragic accident and have no idea that they need to cross over.

And the third reason is fear. From the time of being a small child, everyone hears that if you are not a good person you will go to hell, and because of this some who have crossed over are afraid to take the step into the Summerland, afraid that they may end up in hell.

I believe that you are in death what you are in life. If you are an evil person in life, then you will be an evil person in death. Personally, I can't say that I have run into a mean spirit. However, I was slapped at a cemetery last year after laughing at a name on a headstone ... but if it was in fact paranormal, I deserved it.

I believe that people's minds have opened greatly in the past ten years. I remember at twenty-nine years of age telling people ghost stories, and they looked at me like I was crazy or the devil himself. Now I am sometimes overwhelmed by the number of people who recognize me and want to hear about the paranormal, or want to tell me their own stories. It has caused me to be late to work on more than one occasion.

JOHN TALLON — PARANORMAL INVESTIGATOR

I see the difference between a ghost and a spirit in religious connotations, but not as a paranormal difference.

The most malevolent spirits/ghosts that I have encountered were via EVPs. I would not want to repeat these, as they were blunt, to the point, and quite nasty. These encounters were at prisons, so one would expect more malicious responses in such a location.

I would say that most ghosts/spirits are benevolent. They are holding on to something that they hold dear to themselves, whether that be a piece of land, a memento, a pet, or a family member. I have encountered ghosts/spirits that have remained to oversee the welfare of their families. Even a great-grandmother who watches over the great-grandchild she had never met in life. The way we love and are loved cannot be taken away from us even at the time of our death.

Malevolence, hatred, spite, love, memory, and not knowing that they are deceased are some reasons I believe that ghosts/spirits stay at given locations. The worse the location, the more wicked an encounter is expected. For example, at a prison. Men and women died in assaults and by capital punishment. These are very vicious ways to meet one's end, and to remain and provide similar experiences to others could be the only way that someone could have to extract their pound of flesh.

Benign spirits/ghosts may be looking after or holding on to something that they love without end. They may be looking out for those they love and do not want to let them go.

You often hear a phrase in hospitals similar to, "They are holding on. They should be dead but just keep hanging on." This rips my heart apart! When this person passes away, did they get to do what they were holding on for? Did they see the person that they were waiting for? Did they get to pass away free of wants/needs? If not, how does it affect them after they pass away? Is this one reason that ghosts/spirits visit family members or other loved ones? What causes residual spirits? Why do they stay in their own time frame, oblivious to any changes in the world around them? Is it simply because they do not know that they are deceased, or is there more to it than that?

It is my belief that if a person is in the right place at the right time and has the correct mindset, they can be occupied by a spirit. I have witnessed such an experience. Do I believe malicious spirits/ghosts inhabit human bodies to accomplish their own sinful motives? I cannot say. Exorcism? By faith I should, but by science, I do not know.

If it is a malevolent spirit, one should seek a religious fix. If it is an intelligent haunt, you must try to find what it needs or what it is holding on to/for. Can you provide it satisfaction for its needs? Can you make a deal? As with anyone else with a personal problem, try to reach out to the spirit, establish a dialogue, and try to best provide what you can to satisfy all parties.

Society today is more willing to accept ghosts and hauntings because it is peer-accepted and trendy. More and more television shows put the paranormal in people's faces, so if it is popular on television, then it must be okay. It is this aspect of society's need for acceptance that has brought this topic out of the closets. It started out with one or two television shows, and then more and more appeared, and those who were believers found vindication. It is now all right to say the word *paranormal* without being looked upon as strange.

6

COMMUNICATING WITH SPIRITS

If things start going bump in the night, and you think you might be dealing with a haunting, how do you go about understanding who or what is trying to get your attention … and why?

Or, perhaps it isn't a haunting you want to have solved or ended, but rather communication with a loved one's spirit would bring comfort and reassurance. What would be the best, and worst, way to attempt that?

The following words of wisdom should be heeded.

———

WHAT IS RECOMMENDED?

RONA ANDERSON — PARANORMAL INVESTIGATOR AND PSYCHIC MEDIUM

The best way would be to think of a protective shield spiritually (like white light surrounding you, or knight's armour, or angels and spirit guides to protect you) and then ask if the spirit would please communicate with you, using a voice recorder. Make sure that you also request that this conversation is only with this spirit and is only for your highest good. Ask questions that make sense and not ridiculous ones. If you are trying to communicate with someone you used to know, make sure you ask a specific question that only you and they know the answer to.

———

STEPHEN BOSTON — PARANORMAL INVESTIGATOR AND TECHNICAL TRAINER

Working on the technical side of paranormal investigation, I would personally say EVP sessions are the best way to communicate. These can provide some very interesting results that can be recorded and presented in an evidential form at a later date. We find that EVP is the most common kind of evidence we get from investigations.

———

JILL BRUENER — PSYCHIC, MEDIUM, CLAIRVOYANT, AND SPIRITUAL ADVISOR

Now, some metaphysical people will disagree with me, but I think that automatic writing is a good way to communicate with Spirit, but again, you have to do it the right way. All you need is a pen and paper. I always hold them both and ask that they be blessed by God as an instrument to connect with my highest guide of the white light. Then you can either write down a question or just ask your guide if there is anything that you need to know. The biggest thing with automatic writing is to let go. Don't dwell on it, don't analyze it, don't think you're just making it up, just go with the flow. Sit somewhere where you aren't going to be disturbed. Call in your angels and your highest guides of the white light.

This technique requires time and practice, but eventually you will get the hang of it and they will be able to work with your energy. At first you may get just a word or a phrase, but if you keep at it they will actually write you pages of information. Just go with it. You will be surprised when you read what was written and think, "I don't remember writing that." To me this is a safe and accurate method to communicate with spirit as long as you work in God's light.

Another method of communicating with spirit that I really enjoy is working with a pendulum. These are marvellous little tools to communicate with your guides. To me, again, they are safe as long as you ask it to be blessed to work only with the white light of God. When you buy a pendulum you first want to ask it to show you *yes* and show you *no*. Hold it and say, "Show me *yes*." Most of the time *yes* will be a circular motion, and it will swing in a circle. *No* is usually back and forth and will just swing that way. Remember, if you are not supposed to know something or the outcome has not been determined, the pendulum will usually just sit or perhaps jiggle a bit. Or you need to rephrase the question or define it more.

I love pendulums and I think they're great. As with anything else, you just have to use common sense and be respectful of Spirit. The spirit world is nothing to dabble with or to show disrespect to.

Of course, the best method for me to communicate with Spirit is psychically. I can see them and hear them. Naturally, most people don't have this gift, but it is the most effective spiritual way to have spirit communication. I work with my master guide, Elijah. He is the one that talks to me and shows me things. I also have the ability to communicate directly with ghosts and spirits, which is a huge benefit to me.

———

BARRI GHAI — PARANORMAL INVESTIGATOR

I would prefer to use the latest in ghost-hunting technology to try and communicate with spirits. EMF meters can give real visual results and also provide an insight into the science behind paranormal investigations. The use of digital voice recorders to capture what is known as electronic voice phenomena would top my list of preferred methods of communication with a spirit. The simple act of asking questions and recording their disembodied voices is terrifying and amazing. Recent enhancements to equipment mean we are now able to sometimes listen to these answers in real time and react to them during an investigation.

———

SCOTT HOBBS — PARANORMAL INVESTIGATOR

The best way for us to communicate, by far, has been through audio recordings. While tedious, and sometimes downright boring, nothing comes close to what we have picked up on our audio. We've had investigations where we have left thinking there was nothing to be found, only to find five or six direct answers to our questions picked up on audio.

At one home we investigated, the owner had informed me that a friend once felt like they were physically struck by the spirit in the home. I asked it to slap me, scratch me, or punch me in the face. My teammates found it amusing, but the next day when we went over the audio, a woman's voice clearly responds to me with, "Why?"

———

AMANDA HORLEY — PARANORMAL INVESTIGATOR

I personally prefer to sense as much information about them as I can, and if I am with someone else who is asking questions, I can often "feel" the answers, and I do like this way of working. I will talk to them both out loud and within my head, as I would any person. Spirits don't actually need to hear the sound of your voice.

We have also occasionally had good sessions talking to spirits using either glass divination or table tipping to get answers. In all cases, it is important to treat them with respect and dignity, and not to pry if they don't want to give information about an aspect of their life/death. To me, shouting and threatening is totally unacceptable. We are in their space. Asking spirits to "knock once for yes and twice for no" is also something I prefer not to do. You are then limited to closed questions, and it is incredibly difficult to have a conversation like this.

———

JAMIE JACKSON — PARANORMAL INVESTIGATOR

The best way is by talking directly with the spirits. I always talk to them as if they are real living people. Granted, there is rarely a verbal reply. Recorders also make communicating easier. I have had one or two "conversations" by asking questions and receiving replies in the form of EVPs.

———

KIMBERLEY LAPIERRE — PARANORMAL INVESTIGATOR

The best way to communicate with a spirit is with the help of a medium. This is what they are gifted to do. A medium has the ability to become a conduit for communication between those who have crossed over to the other side and those who are still here on Earth. However, the best way to communicate with a ghost is to talk to them as you would any live person. They have feelings, just like us, and deserve to be treated with respect. We kindly ask them to communicate with us, and most times, they are more than willing to co-operate. We do not agree with some paranormal investigators who feel the need to antagonize ghosts. For whatever reason, they are trapped in their existence, and it is disrespectful and shameful to try and anger them into "performing" for the cameras.

———

DON SWAIN — PARANORMAL INVESTIGATOR

I believe that you should just talk to the spirit, as it is an emotional, intelligent person. Through my work with EVP, I truly believe that a spirit has emotions and is intelligent.

———

WHAT IS NOT RECOMMENDED?

RONA ANDERSON — PARANORMAL INVESTIGATOR AND PSYCHIC MEDIUM

Definitely the worst way to communicate is the Ouija board, because people take no precautions and literally open the door to their house saying, "Come on in, any strange and negative beings."

———

JILL BRUENER — PSYCHIC, MEDIUM, CLAIRVOYANT, AND SPIRITUAL ADVISOR

"I think the worst way to communicate is with a Ouija board.

Yes, the Ouija board is supposedly just a game that is manufactured, but it is also a tool to connect with Spirit. It doesn't matter if it is supposed to be a game, it is more than that. Spirit will use any means available to communicate. Let me try to explain why I am against a novice using the Ouija board.

In most cases, you hear of kids or teenagers thinking it is cool to play with, or try to hold a seance with, the Ouija board. What these immature psychic wannabes don't understand is that they can actually pull in some spirit, and it doesn't have to be a benevolent one. Most of the time they will pull in lower negative energies.

Let's say there is one public phone in Grand Central Station. Thousands of people walk by that phone every day. You may have a businessman, a nurse, a minister, a murderer, a rapist, a thief, a police officer, a nun … the point is, people from every walk of life may walk past that phone.

Let's say you call that telephone and just let it ring. You just dialled this number, and you are waiting for anybody to answer. Eventually someone may walk over and answer the phone. Who will answer? It's a crapshoot. Anybody could, from any walk of life. You could get a nice person or a bad person. You are just taking a chance to see who will answer it. So then you have them on the phone … what do you do? Do you get scared and hang up? Maybe, but they are still on the line.

In essence, you have called this person into you and you have connected with them. You hung up, but they are still there. Just for the sake of argument, let's say their phone has caller ID. They now know who you are and they can call back. You have made a connection with them. We don't just make random calls and hope somebody we know answers the phone. If we call a place of business we ask for a particular person. If we call a friend we dial their personal number so that we make sure to get that person. The Ouija board works like a telephone. If you just say, "Is there anybody out there?" you are going to get just anybody, good or bad. You have to know how to connect with spirit and how to bring in the person with whom you wish to communicate.

Novices don't have a clue. They just set up the board and think they are having great fun. If they make contact it may not be with a good spirit, and they get scared or bored so just quit and put the board away. What they failed to do was "hang up," or break the connection. They have called in a soul, and that soul is now present.

I got a call from a woman once who actually spent the night in her car. Her daughter and a friend had been playing with a Ouija board and brought in a rather foul spirit. It was throwing things around in the house and scaring them to death. She called me over, and I had to do a cleansing and send this spirit back to where it came from.

In simple terms … don't play with a Ouija board if you don't know what you are doing. You can call in all kinds of negative energy.

BARRI GHAI — PARANORMAL INVESTIGATOR

The worst or in my opinion most dangerous way to communicate with a spirit is through the use of Ouija or spirit boards. These devices, made more popular in the 1960s by a large global board game manufacturer, actually do work! The simple act of asking to communicate with a spirit or loved one using a glass or planchette does in fact open an invisible portal or doorway to the spirit realm. This opening then offers any passing spirit the opportunity to enter our world and attach themselves to someone or something.

In almost all cases that I read about or handle, people have either deliberately used a Ouija board or played with it in recent months. This is often the cause of their haunting or current problem.

Other variations of channelling one's energy in this way are also dangerous tools to communicate with a spirit. Dowsing, glass divination, and table tipping all generally thin the gap between our world and the world of spirits. The issue, and cause of much controversy amongst the paranormal community, is whether this is all really dangerous, or has it just been made this way through recent films like *The Exorcist*, etc.?

In my opinion there is something about the act of using a planchette or glass to communicate with ghosts that seems too uncontrolled and borders on black magic and occultism. Is it because I have personally experienced a negative energy as a direct result of playing with this so-called game, or is it more than that? Maybe it is foresight or a psychic sense that warns me away from using the more traditional methods of spirit communication.

JULIE HARWOOD — PARANORMAL INVESTIGATOR

I think if a spirit is going to interact with you then it will, regardless of how you communicate; however, I also know that different people like/dislike different methods of communication. In my opinion, one of the worst ways to communicate is by Ouija board. This is nothing to do with the method itself, just the reaction to the idea of using a

Ouija board. Thanks to the movies and media in general these boards (originally parlour games) have picked up a bad reputation. Because of this, people's expectations when using them are high, and I don't think this is a way an investigator should go into an experiment.

———

DON SWAIN — PARANORMAL INVESTIGATOR

Ouija boards and seances are the worst. I believe that both are just tools to open a portal into another dimension. Any spirit on the other side can tell you exactly what you want to hear, in order to come through the portal.

7

PARTING WORDS

Seeing is believing, but for those who do not have that opportunity, hearing from others who have seen is the next best thing. I understand skepticism as it relates to the paranormal, because it is hard to believe it is really happening even when you are staring right at an apparition. But when it does happen, you never forget it, and you want others to know about it too.

I have seen spirits with my own eyes ... and felt their touch ... and heard their voices. And I have found my own experiences, and those of others, to be awe-inspiring on many levels. It affirms for me, personally, that there is life after death, even if the extent of that reality is beyond my ability to fully understand still. Perhaps therein lies the main appeal of this topic.

It is a fact that our physical life is finite, and therefore we all have the same vested interest in what becomes of our souls, after death.

I give sincere thanks to the paranormal experts who gave so generously of their time and knowledge, and to the many anonymous contributors who shared their own "haunted" experiences and, in doing so, made this book possible.

POSTSCRIPT

If you have had a ghostly/spiritual/haunting experience too, and would like it to be included in my next book (anonymously for privacy), please visit my website for details: *www.dorahlwilliams.com*.

ALSO BY DORAH L. WILLIAMS

Haunted

The Incredible True Story of a Canadian Family's Experience Living in a Haunted House
978-1550023787
$19.99

It was an irrational decision. Despite having just moved into a beautiful new house, the Williams family gave in to an odd, overwhelming desire to purchase and move into a Victorian home they had come upon by chance. They were curious, of course, as to why the house had, in the past, had such a high vacancy rate — no one ever seemed to live in it for a long period of time. But that curiosity didn't last long, because shortly after moving in, strange things began to happen. It became abundantly clear that the home's past owners had all had a reason for leaving: fear. The Williamses' new home was haunted. At first, the family tried telling themselves there were logical explanations for the strange things they all were witnessing. But before long they came to accept the fact that they were sharing their home with ghosts. *Haunted* is the Williams family's story from the point of view of the mother, Dorah. Through her chilling reminiscences, we witness the all-too-real goings-on in the house. And we join the family as they seek a way to bring an end to the paranormal events that were occurring with ever more frequency and intensity, and learn why the events began in the first place.

DUNDURN
www.dundurn.com

Visit us at
Dundurn.com
Definingcanada.ca
@dundurnpress
Facebook.com/dundurnpress